Jean Stafford

Twayne's United States Authors Series

Warren French, Editor

Indiana University, Indianapolis

TUSAS 487

JEAN STAFFORD
(1915–1979)
Photograph courtesy of Pach-Bettmann

Jean Stafford

By Mary Ellen Williams Walsh

Idaho State University

Twayne Publishers • Boston

Jean Stafford

Mary Ellen Williams Walsh

Copyright © 1985 by G.K. Hall & Company

All Rights Reserved
Published by Twayne Publishers
A Division of G.K. Hall & Company
70 Lincoln Street
Boston, Massachusetts 02111

Book Production by Lyda E. Kuth
Book Design by Barbara Anderson

Printed on permanent/durable acid-free
paper and bound in the United States of
America.

Library of Congress Cataloging in Publication Data

Walsh, Mary Ellen Williams.
  Jean Stafford.

  (Twayne's United States authors series; TUSAS 487)
  Bibliography: p. 105
  Includes index.
  1. Stafford, Jean, 1915–1979. 2. Women in literature.
3. Authors, American—20th century—Biography.
I. Title. II. Series.
PS3569.T2Z9   1985   813'.54   [B]   85-5248
ISBN 0-8057-7441-6

Contents

About the Author

Mary Ellen Williams Walsh is professor of English at Idaho State University, where she has taught since 1971, and has also served as associate dean of the College of Liberal Arts and as assistant vice-president for academic affairs. She earned a B.A. in English at North Texas State College and an M.A. and Ph.D. at the University of Arizona. Her publications include articles on nineteenth- and twentieth-century American novelists and *A Vast Landscape: Time in the Novels of Thornton Wilder.*

Preface

Jean Stafford grew up in the West, from her birth in 1915 in Covina, California, to her graduation with both an A.B. and an A.M. from the University of Colorado in Boulder in 1936. She was growing up in a West that was slowly struggling out of its mythicized past into what Stafford perceived as less than a glorious present. Her father helped in the mythicizing process; he wrote western fiction under the pseudonyms of Ben Delight and Jack Wonder. Stafford was determined to leave the West as soon as she could. Her first opportunity came in the academic year 1936–37, when she was awarded a fellowship to study philology in Heidelberg, during Hitler's nazification of the German universities. She made her second opportunity, by fleeing, apparently literally, in the middle of the night on a bus to Boston, after a year and a few months of teaching unhappily in the Midwest. After arriving on that bus in Boston in the fall of 1938, she never again lived farther west than Baton Rouge, Louisiana. Except for the months in Louisiana and a few more months in Tennessee, she lived the rest of her life on the East Coast—in Massachusetts, Connecticut, Maine, and New York. She owned two homes in her life, her prized first house in Damariscotta Mills, Maine, which she bought with the sales of her first novel, and the place she lived longest in her adult life, the house she inherited on Long Island from her third husband. She married three times, first to a poet who would become famous, Robert Lowell. The last time she married a journalist who was already famous, A. J. Liebling. She had no children. She lived very unhappily with Cal Lowell in Maine and elsewhere; she lived happily with Joe Liebling during the few years they had before his death.

This listing of places and people in the life of Jean Stafford is important in a way that is not always true about an author, because Stafford wrote best when she wrote about places and people she had experienced intensely. She said she shared the "sense of place" and "dislocation" of Henry James and Mark Twain.[1] Certainly, in her own work she returned again and again to those places that had been most important in her life—Covina and Boulder, which she called "Adams," Heidelberg, Damariscotta Mills. When her characters have left their homes, they often express in one way or another their sense of dislocation, from the rather direct statements in such stories as "The Bleeding Heart" and "Children Are Bored on Sunday" to the less direct and meditative expressions in such stories as "A Reunion" and "The Lippia Lawn." As these remarks suggest, her fiction is often highly autobiographical. It is her own life as a girl and as a woman that has inspired much of her best work. Her first story, "And Lots of Solid Color" (1939), and the last story published before her death, "An Influx of Poets" (1978), are autobiographical bookends for the work that comes between.

The work that comes between is three novels—*Boston Adventure* (1944), *The Mountain Lion* (1947), and *The Catherine Wheel* (1952)— and nearly fifty stories, plus a substantial body of essays and articles. Most of her nonfiction was published after her marriage to Liebling. She has declared that her happiness with him made her unable to write fiction as she had before. In contrast, her unhappiness with Lowell added substantially to her production of fiction. The fiction and the nonfiction share a major subject—the lives of girls and women, her own life, often thinly disguised, and her vision of the lives of other women. She wrote only nine stories with boys or men as central characters. She included only two of these in *The Collected Stories*. Two boys, Ralph Fawcett and Andrew Shipley, share the focus with Molly Fawcett and Katherine Congreve in *The Mountain Lion* and *The Catherine Wheel*.

The central characters, the girls and women, are usually portrayed as powerless victims—of their poverty or of their wealth, of rejection by people they love, of the roles into which society forces them, of the devalued status of divorcées and even widows, of their own deep anger at their powerless state, of their inability to act, of all these things internalized as self-hatred. Often the relationship to the father is crucial; it is usually ambivalent and sometimes hostile. The orphan, often fatherless, sometimes motherless, is a dominant character type.

This study examines Stafford's work from the perspective that her exploration of the human condition begins with an exploration of what it means to be female. The perspective allows one to demonstrate that themes such as the conflict in values and manners arising from class distinctions and from different cultures, the struggle to achieve maturity and understanding of self, and the isolation of societal misfits develop in a substantially different way when the central figure is female rather than male. Stafford's fiction is examined here in a way in which it may be collectively viewed—as an exploration of the ages of women: childhood and adolescence, young womanhood, maturity and old age.

Early reviewers and later academic critics have made much of the Proustian and Jamesian qualities of Stafford's style and content. She has expressed her admiration of James and Twain. Labeling her work as part of the school of one of the masters, however, can obscure her uniqueness. She did evoke Proust in *Boston Adventure*. She used themes and an intense psychological realism that James had also used. She had a Twainian ear for the colloquial speech of Americans and a Twainian eye for the grittiness of American places. She melded all these elements, however, into a style and into developing a subject matter that was clearly her own. The style is compounded of an ironic detachment, a lucidity in language, a "lapidary speech"[2] studded with words like "oleaginous," "integument," and "machiolations," as well as with the slang and the western language she grew up with, expressed in its own rhythms. Her subject matter, as I have stated above, is the lives of girls and women. And her primary form of expression has been the short story. The excellence of her work in that genre was recognized in 1970 by the award of the Pulitzer Prize for fiction for *The Collected Stories*. The stories, both collected and un-collected, and the best of her novels, *The Mountain Lion*, have gained for Stafford a deserved reputation as a twentieth-century author of considerable distinction.

No biography of Stafford has been published, nor has an extended study of her work. Critical articles have been chiefly concerned with her novels. This study attempts to correct the imbalance. It provides an account of the crucial periods in Stafford's life. It gives major at-tention to her short fiction, both collected and uncollected. It also calls attention to her essays and articles. Not discussed here are the over one hundred book and movie reviews that she wrote. In their great variety, they do not finally develop a particular critical approach to literature that proves useful in evaluating her own work, although individual reviews are cogent and interesting in themselves. The re-views are listed and annotated in Wanda Avila's *Jean Stafford: A Com-prehensive Bibliography*.

Mary Ellen Williams Walsh

Idaho State University

Acknowledgments

The research for this work was partially funded by Grant no. 529 from the Faculty Research Committee, Idaho State University, Pocatello, Idaho.

I wish to thank Nora Quinlan, Sonia Jacobs, and Dinah McKay, who greatly helped me with my work in the Jean Stafford Collection in the Department of Special Collections at the University Libraries, the University of Colorado at Boulder. I also wish to thank Wanda Avila for her bibliographic assistance.

Finally, I wish to acknowledge permission to quote from the following works:

Excerpts from *Boston Adventure* by Jean Stafford, copyright 1944 by Harcourt Brace Jovanovich, Inc.; renewed 1972 by Jean Stafford. Reprinted by permission of the publisher.

Excerpts reprinted by permission of Farrar, Straus and Giroux, Inc., from *Bad Characters,* copyright 1946, 1953, 1954, © 1956, 1957, 1964 by Jean Stafford. *The Catherine Wheel,* copyright 1951, 1952 by Jean Stafford. *Children Are Bored on Sunday,* copyright 1945, 1946, 1948, 1949, 1950, 1953 by Jean Stafford. *The Collected Stories of Jean Stafford,* copyright 1944, 1945, 1946, 1948, 1949, 1950, 1951, 1952, 1953, 1954, © 1955, 1956, 1958, 1964, 1968, 1969 by Jean Stafford. *A Mother in History,* © 1965, 1966 by Jean Stafford. *The Mountain Lion,* copyright 1947, © 1972 by Jean Stafford.

Excerpts from the unpublished manuscript of "In the Snowfall" and a note on "The Echo and the Nemesis" reprinted by permission of the Estate of Jean Stafford Liebling.

Excerpts reprinted by permission of Helen Winter Stauffer and Susan J. Rosowski from "The Young Girl in the West: Disenchantment in Jean Stafford's Short Fiction," by Mary Ellen Williams Walsh, in *Women and Western American Literature,* edited by Helen Winter Stauffer and Susan J. Rosowski, pp. 230–42. Troy, N.Y.: Whitston Publishing Co., 1982.

Chronology

1915   Jean Stafford born in Covina, California, 1 July, youngest of four children of John Richard and Mary Ethel McKillop Stafford.

1921   Moves with family to Colorado.

1925–1932   Attends University Hill School. Graduates from State Preparatory School, Boulder.

1936   Receives A.B., A.M., University of Colorado, Boulder.

1936–1937   Studies philology at the University of Heidelberg.

1937   Introduced during summer to Robert Lowell by Ford Madox Ford, in Boulder.

1937–1938   Instructor, Stephens College, Columbia, Missouri.

1938   Teaches briefly in Iowa. Moves to Concord, Massachusetts. Badly injured in automobile accident in car driven by Robert Lowell.

1939   First story, "And Lots of Solid Color."

1940   Marries Robert Lowell, 2 April.

1940–1941   Secretary for *Southern Review* in Baton Rouge while Lowell attends graduate school.

1941–1942   Secretary at Sheed and Ward in New York.

1942–1943   With Lowell, lives in Tennessee with Allen Tate and Caroline Gordon.

1943   July–September, works on *Boston Adventure* at Yaddo, Sarasota Springs, New York.

1944   *Boston Adventure*. Receives *Mademoiselle*'s Merit Award for Outstanding Achievement. *Boston Adventure* selected by the People's Book Club.

1945   Awarded Guggenheim Fellowship and National Institute of Arts and Letters Grant. Buys house in Damariscotta Mills, Maine.

1946   Separates from Robert Lowell.

1947   *The Mountain Lion.* Spends most of year as patient at Payne Whitney Clinic, New York.

1948   Divorces Robert Lowell. Awarded Guggenheim Fellowship and National Press Club Award.

1949   Travels in Europe on assignment for the *New Yorker.*

1950   Marries Oliver Jensen, 28 January. Delivers the Sophie Hart Lecture, Wellesley College.

1952   *The Catherine Wheel.* Addresses 1952 Writer's Conference in the Rocky Mountains, University of Colorado, Boulder.

1953   Divorces Oliver Jensen. *Children Are Bored on Sunday* and *The Interior Castle.*

1955   Receives O. Henry Award, First Prize, for "In the Zoo."

1956   Meets A. J. Liebling in London. Awarded the Norlin Medal, University of Colorado, Boulder.

1959   Marries A. J. Liebling, 3 April.

1962   *The Lion and the Carpenter* and *Elephi, the Cat with the High I.Q.* Serves on the jury for the National Book Award for fiction.

1963   Travels in Europe with Liebling in fall. Widowed by Liebling's death on 21 December.

1964   *Bad Characters.*

1964–1965   Fellow at the Center for Advanced Studies, Wesleyan University.

1965   Awarded Rockefeller Foundation Grant.

1966   *A Mother in History* and *Selected Stories.*

1967–1973   Adjunct professor at Columbia University.

1969   *The Collected Stories.* Awarded Ingram-Merrill Grant and Chapelbrook Grant.

1970   Receives Pulitzer Prize for fiction for *The Collected Stories.* Elected to membership in National Academy of Arts and Letters. Writer in Residence, Wesleyan University.

1971   Delivers the Barnard Lectures, Barnard College.

1972   Awarded L.H.D., University of Colorado, Boulder.

1973   Awarded Litt.D., Southampton College.

1975   Serves on jury for Pulitzer Prize for fiction.

1976   Suffers stroke, which results in aphasia.

1979   Dies at White Plains, New York, 26 March.

Chapter One
Life and Art

From West to East

Jean Stafford was born and bred a westerner, but "hot-footed" it to Europe and to the East as soon as she was able. Her choice, in 1969, of the verb to describe her leavetaking indicates that her ties to the West and its vernacular stayed near, if not dear, to her regardless of the many places where she hung her hat in later years.

Stafford was born in Covina, California, on 1 July 1915, to John Richard and Mary Ethel McKillop Stafford. She was the youngest of four children, with two older sisters, Mary Lee and Marjorie, and a brother, Dick. Her father, under the pen names of Jack Wonder and Ben Delight, wrote western stories and at least one novel, *When Cattle Kingdom Fell* (1907). He once worked as a reporter for the *Chicago Sun* and for a newspaper in New York City. In California, during Stafford's early childhood, he was a rancher. During World War II, he worked as a carpenter in the Portland, Oregon, shipyards. His father had been a cattle rancher in the Texas Panhandle and later in Missouri. As a boy in Missouri, John Stafford claimed, he had seen Jesse James. Stafford's mother, "Miss Pink" McKillop, was the daughter of Malcolm McKillop, Esq. Att'y. She grew up in the tiny Missouri town of Rockport, where she and John Richard Stafford were married on 26 June 1907.

Stafford gave glimpses of her childhood in California in essays primarily concerned with other topics. In Covina, the Staffords' house had a lippia lawn and was bordered by a grove of English walnuts, as is the Fawcetts' in *The Mountain Lion*. Stafford's first remembered Christmas there, when she was four or five, left her with a lifelong feeling of loss, which overshadowed the joy she felt from receiving the only beautiful gift her father's mother bestowed on the four Stafford children that year. Recalling the experience, she writes, "My joy came not only from the conviction that I had been singled out and grandly forgiven—if, that is, I had ever been recognized in the first place—but from the charming, treasurable beauty of my little bag."

The lingering sense of loss came from her actually losing the little bag the same afternoon. Christmas, then, for her began every later year with her "futile prowl through the mustard yellow depot at Covina" and over and over through the other spots she went that day. She found herself, she says, looking in the streets of Freiburg im Breisgau, "on luminous lawns in Louisiana," in Maine, in the mountains of Tennessee, and in the streets of Beacon Hill.[1] Stafford also recalled that at five she "had to wear a taffeta Mackenzie hair ribbon and sing 'Comin' Thro' the Rye' for the pleasure of a Presbyterian pastor in California recently uprooted from Dundee."[2]

The Stafford family moved to Colorado from California when Stafford was five, after having left Covina to live a short time in San Diego. By 1925, the family had settled in Boulder, where Stafford attended the University Hill School and where she began to write, as soon as she could, at six. It was then she wrote the poem "Gravel, gravel on the ground," which she later assigned to Molly in *The Mountain Lion*. At eight, she wrote a long story on kidnapping, "The Unsuccessful Amateur."[3] The heroes of the stories she wrote between the ages of eight and ten were "daring, dashing, tall in the saddle and easy on the eye. . . . To a man, they had steely-blue eyes to match the barrels of their Colt .45s."[4]

A major influence on her early writing was reading the dictionary. "My language was incredible," she recalled. "I remember in one of my stories writing that a man had *oleaginous* black hair. I somehow managed to get hold of a Smith Premier typewriter; it had eight banks and looked like an organ. That was when I was about eleven."[5] Also at eleven, Stafford scavenged in the Boulder city dump and behind the University of Colorado fraternity houses for empty, returnable Coca-Cola bottles, so that she could finance her illicit Coke habit (her mother had forbidden her the drink), and thereby undoubtedly picked up the bacteria that led to a host of childhood illnesses.[6]

Some of Stafford's most vivid childhood memories of Boulder were "a commingling of affection and revulsion": at eleven, learning to shuffle cards from a friend who could play six kinds of solitaire, being frightened on Halloween by having a chamois glove stuffed with wet corn meal extended to her for her to shake, and—the one most vividly described by Stafford and one she used in "Bad Characters"— "the image of a yellow trolley car that used to proceed carefully down from the top of Mapleton Hill and up University Hill until it reached the Chautauqua and there it paused, exhausted, for a long and silent time while the conductor and the passengers got out and ritualistically drank at the water fountain in the shelter house as if this were a spa and they had taken a trolley ride to the cure." She saw her first writer, Robert Frost, the summer she was twelve, when she was working as a maid in a lodge in Boulder Canyon where Frost was a guest.[7]

Stafford had a certain uneasiness in her childhood that is partly explained by what she wrote of a fantasy in which she indulged:

As a Western child, whose daily prospect was of a titanic landscape, of mountains that stretched—peak and chasm and hummock of purple rock— miles beyond vision, and as a contrary child who wished for something altogether other, I lived in my fancy upon an island in the bright blue sea. Its dimensions were those of the mesa in the foothills above our town where I went after school to cogitate until the sun went down; it was no bigger than two city blocks, small enough for me to survey the whole of it from any point. . . .

My gifted eyes . . . uprooted the yucca and the sage and raised a garden of unheard of flowers and a palm tree with a monkey in it. And where the forest ranger's old white horse had walked, I saw the footprints of my own Friday.[8]

The fantasy resulted from her sense that "the Rocky Mountains were too big to take in, too high to understand, too domineering to love; the very spaciousness of the range and of the limitless prairies to the east turned me claustrophobic; they baffled my eye, humiliated me in my picayune stature, and out of self-respect I had to make them vanish and to reduce the world to a rational arena where I knew, at all times, what was going on."[9] In *The Mountain Lion,* Molly and Ralph feel the same overwhelming sense of the Colorado landscape that Stafford here describes.

John Richard Stafford's lack of financial success made it necessary for Stafford's mother to open a boardinghouse in Boulder for students at the University of Colorado. In 1946, Stafford told Eileen Simpson that she had "loathed cleaning for and serving others, had resented her family's poverty and had felt kinship only with her brother Dick, to whom she was very close."[10] Thirty years later, she reiterated that she "was filled with resentment at my poverty, at having to serve tables."[11] At about the same time, she told Wilfrid Sheed about dreaming for eight consecutive nights about a family breakfast in Colorado, in which the sun shone and all the family smiled at her and which caused her to say, "If I have that dream again, I'll go ab-so-lutely crazy." Sheed's interpretation of her response was that "she hated the people at that table, but whether for something they'd taken away or for something that was never there, I don't think even she knew, or wanted to know."[12] In this family situation, Stafford finished high school and entered college, graduating from the State Preparatory School in Boulder in 1932, and entering the University of Colorado the following fall.

In a memoir of her college years, "Souvenirs of Survival," Stafford only indirectly describes her family's situation. She recounts that she had won a scholarship to pay her annual tuition. She bought her books and paid her fees from the savings from her summer job "at a dude camp in the mountains where [she] . . . worked as chambermaid and waitress for twenty-five dollars a month plus tips (and board with the wranglers, who despised the dudes, and room in a vaguely renovated henhouse). . . ." In addition, she had the "best-paying" job for an undergraduate on campus: "I was the model for the life drawing and painting class and I was paid seventy-five cents an hour. For three hours in the morning, two days a week, I stood with all my weight on the ball of one hand, 'undraped,' as it was decorously described, in a chilly tower room where I was grimily sketched in charcoal and viscously painted in oil."[13] The summer job is the one Kitty Winstanley grimly recalls in "The Tea Time of Stouthearted Ladies." Cora Savage, in "The Philosophy Lesson," models as Stafford did while the story unfolds.

Most of Stafford's friends at the university were poor and also worked their way through school by whatever jobs they could pick up. To the Greek-letter sororities and fraternities to which they did not belong, they were known as "barbarians." Lacking a glittering social life, they spent much of their time drunk on three-point-two beer and the ideas that they were encountering in newly discovered writers. Among their escapades was driving recklessly and not very soberly through the mountains around Boulder, during which, on one occasion, they encountered a mountain lion in the foothills above the town. Above all, "landlocked, penniless, ragtag, and bobtail, [they] planned splendid odysseys," primarily to Europe.[14] Stafford, at least, was able to realize her dream.

Stafford entered the university to read philosophy, but by her third year had become interested in the Middle Ages and had begun the study of medieval languages. She graduated in 1936 with both an A.B. and an A.M., having written her master's thesis on "Profane and Divine Love in English Literature of the Thirteenth Century." In her last year at the University of Colorado, she applied for and received a fellowship for the 1936–37 academic year at the University of Heidelberg to study under Johannes Hoops, the famed Anglo-Saxon scholar.

Stafford arrived in Heidelberg in the midst of the nazification of the German universities and endured the "Heil, Hitler" with which each class began and ended. Nonetheless, Stafford later wrote:

No matter what I have subsequently felt about Germany, I shall be glad all my life that I was there at that particular and alarming time. . . . [S]ometimes, obediently raising my right hand and hailing the Fuehrer when I greeted the chambermaid of my pension or the conductor of a trolley car, I felt cowardly and frivolous. . . . But at twenty-one one's noblest attitudes and strictest opinions can be so easily modified: in five minute's walk I could be remote from all evidences of the NSDAP and could find myself on a path in a beautiful and evil and magical forest. I had, in a sense, cheated the depression for the time being. . . . [15]

In Heidelberg, Stafford lived in the Hotel Haarlass, where formerly postulants of the nearby abbey were tonsured. She spent much of her time at a veranda café at the Haarlass, "studying haphazardly, playing amateurish bridge, looking at the mists that half concealed and half disclosed [the] prospect of the distant castle and of the church steeples of Heidelberg, and seeing, from time to time, the sleek black limousines of the Nazi big bugs speeding along the highway." Among her acquaintances was a "rich young American . . . [who] used to give little parties in the private dining room [of the Café Sö], ordering lobster sent from Hamburg and champagne from Alsace."[16] He was to serve as the model for Ian Ferguson in "My Blithe, Sad Bird."

In the summer following her year in Heidelberg, Stafford returned to Boulder to attend a writing school. There Ford Madox Ford introduced her to Robert Lowell, at that time an undergraduate in transition from Harvard to Kenyon College. She spent the academic year 1937–38 at Stephens College in Columbia, Missouri, where she taught freshman English, which was called "Communications," and incidentally gained the material for "Caveat Emptor." Stafford was acidulous in her comments on her experience at Stephens:

> I was frequently summoned to the office of the head of the department or, more terrifyingly, to a dean's office for hurting students' feelings by asking them to come to class in something other than their sleeping pajamas and to refrain from knitting while I was demonstrating subjunctives on the blackboard. . . . There was a "grooming clinic" on the campus . . . and in my communications classes, when I gave an assignment in composition on an open topic, I was often presented with themes titled "A Short History of Fingernail Polish," or "How I Managed My Oily Hair on My Summer Vacation." On Conversation Day, I scarcely had to say a word because those bubbling lasses were so keen on swapping their opinions of the Duchess of Windsor, the dos and don'ts of rearing children, the wisdom of Dale Carnegie and whether miniature golf was here to stay. [17]

The following fall, 1938, when she began teaching at Iowa, where she was enrolled in the Writer's Workshop, she found no greater affinity with her students than she had at Stephens. She left Iowa on a bus in the middle of the night in midsemester when she found that she had in class both a Mr. Mahoney and a Mr. O'Mahoney: "That made her understand once and for all, she said, how ridiculous the whole business was." [18]

The bus from Iowa took her straight to Boston, where she arrived with one third of a manuscript and where she was introduced to several publishers by Howard Mumford Jones. She rented a room in Concord, where she lived for a year. [19] During the fall, she renewed her acquaintance with Robert Lowell with a disastrous consequence. On 22 December 1938, returning drunk from a Boston nightclub, Lowell lost control of the car in which he and Stafford were riding, crashing it in a dead-end street in Cambridge. Stafford was badly hurt in the accident. Her face was disfigured, requiring extensive reconstructive surgery, the agony of which she described in "The Interior Castle," and she suffered internal injuries that apparently prevented her from bearing children. Despite the accident, a courtship between Stafford and Lowell blossomed during the course of a suit for $25,000 in damages for her head injuries that Stafford brought against him. [20] The suit did nothing to endear Stafford to Lowell's parents, who always considered he married beneath his class and during the marriage refused to treat her as a family member, often even intentionally embarrassing and belittling her. [21]

Stafford and Lowell were married on 2 April 1940, in New York at St. Mark's in the Bowery, shortly before he graduated from Kenyon College. The next fall they moved to Louisiana, where she worked as secretary for the *Southern Review* while he attended graduate school at Louisiana State University. Beginning in September 1941, both Stafford and Lowell worked for eight months for the publishing house of Sheed and Ward in New York. Lowell, who had converted to Catholicism while they were in Louisiana, insisted during this time that Stafford, herself a lapsed convert, do some "Catholic work." After frightening experiences traveling to the offices of the *Catholic Worker,* she ended by working in a "friendship house" in Harlem, an episode she later described in "An Influx of Poets."[22]

During these two years, Stafford was also at work on the first novel she would publish, *Boston Adventure,* which appeared in 1944. With an advance from Harcourt Brace, she continued to work on it during a stay of several months in 1942 and 1943 with Caroline Gordon and Allen Tate in Tennessee and during July and August 1943 at Yaddo, the writer's colony in Sarasota Springs, New York, where she shared a bathroom, and little else, with Carson McCullers, and where she apparently suffered a slight nervous breakdown.[23] In September 1943, Lowell declared himself a conscientious objector and was sent to prison in October. Stafford spent the first of those months in New York, visiting Lowell once a week at the Federal Correctional Center in Danbury, Connecticut. When Lowell was paroled to work at a hospital in Bridgeport, Stafford found an apartment for them in Black Rock, Connecticut, in a house that became the setting for "The Home Front."

Boston Adventure was a best-seller. With her profits, Stafford bought her first house, in September 1945, in the small village of Damariscotta Mills, Maine. After spending a few weeks starting the repairs and renovation on the house, Stafford and Lowell went again to stay with the Tates in Tennessee. From mid-January to March 1946, they lived in Cambridge with Delmore Schwartz. In March Stafford moved back to Maine, with Lowell spending time there between frequent trips to New York. During these months, Stafford completed *The Mountain Lion,* which was published in 1947, and Lowell worked on *Lord Weary's Castle.* Given the later relative fame of the husband and wife, it is an interesting footnote that it was Stafford, already established as the author of *Boston Adventure,* who asked her editor, Robert Giroux, if he would be interested in looking at her husband's book.[24] Lowell was almost unknown at the time, having published one volume of poetry privately.

During the long spring at Damariscotta Mills, Stafford and Lowell's marriage, which had always been stormy, began to disintegrate. While they were living in Louisiana, Lowell had broken Stafford's nose again by hitting her in the face.[25] Just as the husband does in "A Country Love Story," Lowell kept himself closed up in his study, between the frequent bouts of bickering that were often occasioned by Stafford's drinking.[26]

The attempt to escape through alcohol remained with Stafford throughout her life. On the night during which her third husband, A. J. Liebling, died in a New York hospital, Stafford attended a cocktail party where she first met Dick Cavett, who describes her presence there "as a highly developed penchant for seeking escape." He found her that evening "one of the funniest and most brilliant women I would ever meet. Also one of the drunkest." After a later night that Stafford spent as the Cavett's houseguest, Cavett asked her "if she thought she *could* stop drinking. She stared out the side window for a long moment without speaking. Then she said in a tone that was neither offended nor melodramatic but chillingly matter-of-fact, 'I loathe alcohol. It is my enemy. And my seducer.' "[27]

In the summer of 1946, Stafford and Lowell entertained many visiting poets at Damariscotta Mills, a time she describes in "An Influx of Poets." That summer Stafford was at work on her third novel—about a suicide that occurred while she was in college. She told the visiting John Berryman and his wife, Eileen Simpson, that she was having great difficulty with it, and she eventually abandoned the project.[28] She ultimately developed the material as a story, "A Philosophy Lesson," rather than as a novel. By the end of the summer, Lowell had begun an affair with Gertrude Buckman, Delmore Schwartz's former wife, and Stafford and Lowell separated in September 1946.[29]

The months immediately following their separation were desperate ones for Stafford. She traveled west, spent eight days in a mental hospital in Detroit, traveled back and forth from Chicago to Denver, and finally lived for a time in a dingy hotel in Greenwich Village. In early 1947, admitting her psychological collapse, she had herself committed to the Payne Whitney Clinic in New York. She spent most of a year there under treatment for conversion hysteria, deep depression, and anxiety.[30] In October 1947, she published a highly poetic account—paralleling her progress toward health with the progress through the seven mansions to the interior castle of St. Teresa of Avila—of her struggle with the insomnia that had begun during her last months with Lowell and accompanied the traumas of the following months.[31] Stafford and Lowell were finally divorced in 1948, after she spent the obligatory six weeks at St. Thomas in the Virgin Islands.

In 1945, Stafford had received a Guggenheim Fellowship and an American Academy and National Institute of Arts and Letters grant. In 1948, she received another Guggenheim Fellowship and a National Press Club Award. These distinctions were followed in later years by the First Prize O. Henry Award in 1955, a Rockefeller Foundation Grant in 1965, and an Ingram-Merrill grant and a Chapelbrook grant in 1969.

On 28 January 1950, Stafford entered a second, and brief, marriage—to Oliver Jensen, once a senior editor for *Life*. In 1952, she published her third novel, *The Catherine Wheel*, the setting for which is based on the Kavanagh mansion, which is located next to Stafford's house in Damariscotta Mills. In the winter of 1953, she once again spent six weeks in the Virgin Islands, to obtain her second divorce. As before, when this marriage ended, she was ill. She spent most of this second time in the islands with Nancy Flagg and her husband, recuperating from a hysterectomy as well as from the emotional upset of the divorce. While she was there, she also wrote "In the Zoo," for which she received the First Prize O. Henry Award.[32]

In 1953, she published the first of the collections of her stories, *Children Are Bored on Sunday*. Her short fiction had been appearing regularly since 1944 in such magazines as the *Partisan Review, Harper's,* and the *New Yorker*. In 1947, she had entered into an agreement with the *New Yorker* for the magazine to have first reading rights to her stories. Her editor was Katherine White, and the arrangement continued for over a decade. Her stories, published generally at the rate of two to four a year, represent her major imaginative production from the mid-fifties through the late sixties. The second collection, *Bad Characters,* was published in 1964; a third, *Selected Stories,* in 1966. In 1970, Stafford received the Pulitzer Prize for her *Collected Stories,* published in 1969.

On 3 April 1959, Stafford married her third husband, A. J. Liebling, the famed journalist. They had met in London three years previously through the offices of Katherine White, where during a summer filled with trips to race tracks all over England, they had begun "a classic romance." By January 1957, when Liebling returned briefly to New York, Stafford was Liebling's "official girl," although he was not yet divorced from his second wife.[33] During their marriage, Stafford entered a low period of productivity. She published no fiction between 1959 and 1964 except two juvenile books, *Elephi, the Cat with the High I.Q.* and *The Lion and the Carpenter and Other Tales from the Arabian Nights Retold.* Stafford said of this time: "I could never figure out why it happened. Perhaps it's too simple an explanation, but I was happy for the first time in my life. [Joe] thought that if I wasn't writing, it meant I was unhappy with him."[34] They did have happy times, but by July 1960 they had begun to go their separate ways. Stafford tired of Liebling's sporting buddies and renewed her literary friendships. They also quarreled over her drinking.[35] They were frequently separated by Liebling's trips to cover stories, but in the late summer and early fall of 1963 they traveled together again in Europe. Liebling died in December 1963.

After Liebling's death, Stafford made her home, until her own death, at the house at East Hampton on Long Island that Liebling had first bought in the thirties. Stafford established herself there as the increasingly crotchety "Widow Liebling."[36] In 1968 she signed a contract with Farrar, Straus and Giroux for an autobiographical novel, "The Parliament of Women," which remained unpublished at her death. Two excerpts from the manuscript have been published as stories, "An Influx of Poets" and "Woden's Day." During the sixties and seventies, Stafford published numerous journalistic pieces, one of them a book, *A Mother in History,* the story of Lee Harvey Oswald's mother. Her work in such magazines as *Vogue, McCall's, Esquire,* and *Mademoiselle* ranges from straightforward interviews with personalities such as Katherine Graham to satirical pieces such as "The Crossword Puzzle Has Gone to Hell." She also wrote numerous book reviews for *Esquire* and *Vogue* and reviewed children's books for the Christmas edition of the *New Yorker* from 1970 to 1976. In 1970, Stafford was made a member of the National Academy of Arts and Letters. In 1975 she served on the jury for the Pulitzer Prize for fiction, as she had earlier served, in 1962, on the jury for the National Book Awards.

In December 1976 Stafford suffered a stroke that resulted in aphasia, surely the cruelest fate for an ardent conversationalist and for a writer who at eleven used *oleaginous* accurately. She died on 26 March 1979 of cardiac arrest at Burke Rehabilitation Center in White Plains, New York. She is inurned beside Joe Liebling at Greenriver Cemetery in East Hampton.

Truth in Fiction

In a 1966 essay, "Truth in Fiction," Stafford made the following observations about the experience of being a writer:

If we are worth our salt, we're scared, and a good deal of the time we should be. But some of the time we're scared of scarecrows—we're scared of fashion: do we parse in the grammars of Freud or Camp or *The New York Review of Books?* From one moment to the next we don't know whether it's "in" or "out" to be afraid of Virginia Woolf.

The only way to disperse these hobgoblins is to write for yourself and God and a few close friends, and if you meet the exacting demands of this group and get their imprimatur, you can devote your whole attention to the really important agony of getting through a writing day.[37]

Despite what she might have feared (quite likely with tongue in cheek) about current tides in the literary world, Stafford chose to write in a style notably free from the experiments in form that characterize much of the literature of the twentieth century. One would have to agree with her own evaluation of *Boston Adventure,* that it is "old-fashioned; it's filled with digressions, for example."[38] But little else that she has written can be considered old-fashioned. The work is traditional in form, but the best of it has the solid stamp of the modern in its symbols, its irony, and its particular awareness of the rueful, as well as of the tragic. It is also demonstrably American, with certain shadings from Mark Twain and Henry James, who, she has written, are two of her "favorite American writers and to whose dislocation and whose sense of place" she feels allied.[39]

In "Truth in Fiction," Stafford also discusses the difficulty of writing too close to the truth of life as it is lived: "while autobiography is inevitable, we must winnow carefully and add a portion of lies, the bigger the better." She recounts her several years' struggle to write about the suicide she had witnessed when she was in college, "the shocking event that had altered the whole course of my existence." By trying to describe it exactly as it happened, she finally discovered, she says, "I was everywhere hampered by the conviction that I must not alter the facts, that I must tell the truth, and nothing but the truth and the *whole* truth, that every act must come in its proper chronological order. . . ." In the same essay, however, Stafford also discusses how she wrote "The Interior Castle": "directly out of experience, adding only a few camouflaging details and subtracting very little."[40] It is the story of her own painful hospital experience following the disfiguring automobile accident in 1938.

As these two examples indicate, Stafford's cautions about "truth" in fiction and about using autobiography are frequently contradicted in her own stories and novels. When Stafford wrote at her best, she was usually writing autobiographically, frequently with few "lies" thrown in and occasionally with the story an almost absolute transcription of actual events in her life, as she acknowledges about the writing of "The Interior Castle." In 1971, when she was at Barnard to give the Barnard Lectures, she told an interviewer: "The stories are generally from direct experience. Each one had at least a seed of truth, though they are not necessarily truths. Some were taken from reality, some from dreams, or even suggested by a single word."[41] Stafford, in fact, drew heavily on the events of her own life in shaping her fiction, so heavily at times that one is tempted to use the phrase "confessional fiction" to describe much of her writing, in much the same sense that Robert Lowell's poetry has been called "confessional."

In 1952 Stafford told an interviewer that "it was the impact of her own frustrations and sufferings engendered by her childhood that has illumined her understanding and deepened her compassion for . . . children."[42] The painful experiences of the young heroines of the stories set in Adams, Colorado, are for the most part developed from Stafford's actual experiences—and, as she indicates, her emotional responses to those experiences—of growing up in Boulder. Her stories about young girls have a particular poignancy that is partly explained by her remark that "my theory about children is my theory about writing. The most important thing in writing is irony, and we find irony most clearly in children. The very innocence of a child is irony. Irony, I feel, is a very high form of morality."[43] In the author's note to *Bad Characters,* Stafford implies that Emily Vanderpool was a victim and acknowledges, "I often occupied her skin."[44] Kitty Winstanley and Cora Savage, college students in the Adams stories, are notably autobiographical; the details of their lives are those of Stafford's own as she describes them in her essay "Souvenirs of Survival."

Stafford's year in Heidelberg is re-created in many stories. Her unhappy time with Lowell in Damariscotta Mills resulted in very thinly fictionalized accounts, most notably in "An Influx of Poets," where little about those months is changed except the names of the people. Finally, her own sense of her self in dislocation, that quality she recognized in Twain and James, accounts for other works. The pain of that dislocation and the resentment she felt first about the early circumstances of her family and later about her marriage to Lowell prevail in the development of many of her autobiographical characters and extend to others who are not strictly tied to her own life.

According to Eileen Simpson, because of her family background Stafford "had wanted desperately to be an orphan. If she bristled when Mrs. Lowell pointed out that she came from a barbarous section of the country, and from parents 'one hadn't heard of,' Jean also cringed because her own judgment coincided with her mother-in-law's."[45] Whether Simpson's facts are straight and her analysis correct, it is indeed a fact of Stafford's fiction that the most dominant character figure is the orphan. Stafford published over forty stories and three novels. Over a third of the stories and all of the novels revolve around orphaned characters. If, as Simpson suggests, Stafford wished to be an orphan so that she might choose who her parents were, her use of the orphan figure can be seen as her exploration of that possibility. One story, "The Bleeding Heart," turns directly on the situation of a young woman, who is not an orphan, wishing, because of her shame at her father, that she were one and that she could be adopted by someone she could respect. Sonia, in *Boston Adventure,* longs to leave her own family and be adopted by Miss Pride. Most of the true orphan figures, however, are revealed as doubly victimized— by being both orphans and female, as most of them are.

All the novels and by far the greater number of the stories center on heroines of different ages. Through the girls and women who predominate as her central characters, Stafford very subtly reveals that themes such as the conflict in values and manners arising from class distinctions and from different cultures, the struggle to achieve maturity and understanding of self, the isolation of social misfits—all develop in a substantially different way when the central figure is female rather than male. The humor that flashes in some of her work and the irony that pervades much of it grow from Stafford's profound consciousness of the limitations of being female—the consciousness from which her broader perception of the human condition grows. There is also often in her work, however, profound bitterness and resentment at the victimization experienced by girls and women. Finally, in some works there is an arrogance and retaliation against those who have done the victimizing. The victimizers are often, in fact, other women. Stafford writes with particular vehemence against her women characters who are landladies or boardinghouse keepers, as her mother was, and against the women who are foster parents of orphans.

The Other Gender

In developing male characters, Stafford places them in situations and settings that are not significantly different from those of her female characters. She frequently portrays them as displaced persons of a kind. She also often shows them at the mercy of a dominating female foster parent or landlady.

The youngest of these, in "A Summer Day" (1948), is an orphaned eight-year-old Indian boy, Jim Littlefield, who is shipped west to Oklahoma when his remaining relative, his grandmother, dies. An apparently well-meaning minister promises him that his "Uncle Sam" will now take care of him. Faced with the heat and the rampant disease at the boarding school to which he is taken, he decides immediately to escape.[46] This decision, although he does not carry it out and the story ends with him sleeping in a fetal position dreaming of his mother, separates him from the orphaned girls in Stafford's fiction, who generally accept their fates and do not expect to escape— and usually are unable even to fantasize about such a possibility.

Clyde, the orphaned young man in "A Slight Maneuver" (1947), has just reached the age at which he has achieved financial freedom from his guardian aunt, Naomi Heath, but he remains subject to her domination. Theo, who is engaged to marry him, realizes at the end of a blissful summer spent on the aunt's dude ranch, that what his aunt requires of him is more important to Clyde than what Theo wishes of him. A disastrous trip to Carlsbad Caverns, mandated by the aunt on the day Theo is to leave, drives from Theo whatever illusions she might have had left about Clyde. In parting at the train, Theo "who died hard and died always with her boots on," taunts Clyde not to forget the vermouth, an errand his aunt has set for him on this their last day together.[47]

The folly and viciousness of landladies disturb and even destroy the lives of male characters in two Heidelberg stories and in one story set in America. In "The Cavalier" (1949), Duane is a nineteen-year-old student at the University of Heidelberg, sent there by his family in hopes that he will overcome his appalling shyness. He has been dismissed over the telephone by the girl he loves (with a remark of the kind that Stafford delights in): "Go peddle your corn." Although he is as lonely and friendless in Heidelberg as he had been in Arizona, his landlady, Fräulein Schmetzer, insists that he is wealthy and well favored like all Americans with numerous girlfriends. She thereby forces him into going out several nights a week to keep up the charade, even though he develops a bad fever and cough. When, in his weakened physical condition, he is brought home by a policeman who also considers him "a young, rich, drunken American," Duane is unable to do other than acquiesce when Fräulein, who has abused his spirits and his health, exclaims, "Oh, the gay blade! Now he has done everything! A duel, is it?"[48]

While Duane is persecuted by what is primarily the folly of Fräulein Schmetzer, combined, however, with her obvious envy and probable hatred of Americans more financially secure than she, Ian Ferguson, in "My Blithe, Sad Bird" (1957), has a much more complex relationship with his Heidelberg landlady. Ian is in truth a rich young American: "He drove a red Mercedes; his Egyptian cigarettes were monogrammed; he hired halls in Heidelberg in which he entertained at midnight dancing and supper parties; he hunted grouse in Yorkshire and roe deer in Bavaria; he bet on the horses at Ostend, gambled regularly at the Kurhaus in Baden-Baden, and sat in a box at La Scala."[49] The baroness adores his grand manner and the style it brings into her dilapidated villa, because it supports "her belief that as long as there were people like him left, there was the possibility that the old order [under which she lived her earlier life] might one day be restored to the world."[50] Ian treats her as his confidant. He admires her stories of her grander days, paying homage to her with treats of aquavit and caviar and gifts of beautiful flowers.

Twenty years later, Miranda Grierson, who had also roomed at the villa, returns to Heidelberg and discovers that Ian Ferguson has bought the villa and lives there with the baroness on their shared dreams of past glory, Ferguson himself now a poor man after having recklessly spent his fortune. The relationship between the two remains ambiguous to Miranda. When the baroness fondly remarks, "You see, there was something about my humble villa by the river that always drew him back," Ferguson replies: "It was the noble lady who lived there that drew me back." Perhaps the baroness has served as surrogate for the mother Ian had worshipped and had lost. Perhaps she is "his waning, paling ladylove." Her hold on him, however, is relentless and grotesque and pathetic. He remains in a "reluctant exile," because, he confides to Miranda, "I'd worry if I left her alone."[51]

"The Home Front" (1945) centers on the harassment of a displaced German Jewish doctor by his Hungarian landlady and her son. Like many of Stafford's characters, he was once a student at Heidelberg. Set in a bleak Connecticut town devoted to war industries, a setting with which Stafford became familiar during the months Lowell was on parole, the story follows the development of the doctor's love for a cat, Milenka, the only thing in his life he has to care for. The developing tension, "as killing a hatred . . . as though they were two jungle beasts, determined to destroy each other,"[52] between himself and the Horvath family over the presence of the cat works itself out in vicious anti-Semitic remarks by the landlady and by the doctor's trying to prevent the capture of birds by the son. It ends when Mr. Horvath shoots Milenka. Unable to do so for Milenka, Dr. Pakheiser gives a "sea burial" to one of the Horvath boy's captured orioles, which, having freed itself, has then got caught and has died in the doctor's chimney. This act fills him with exhilaration. It also frees him from the murderous vengefulness of his enemies that could have ensnared him and brought him into a corresponding viciousness.

The women in the stories just discussed come to their domineering and oppressive roles from their own unhappy situations. Fräulein Schmetzer, who torments Duane, is a "panicky spinster" forced to take in lodgers, but able to rent only the room in which Duane lives, where "everything was missing in one part or broken in another, spotted or faded if it was a fabric, scratched if it was made of marble or porcelain."[53] It is the pathos of her own life that leads her to fantasize for Duane a glamour she can never hope to attain. The widowed baroness is to Miranda Grierson the "very crystallization of pathos." Having once partaken in a grand, aristocratic life, she is now reduced to a state in which her "bright-blue eyes were frantic and [her] thin hands trembled in perpetual anxiety."[54] Mrs. Horvath, with little else to excuse her behavior, is herself a displaced person. Naomi Heath, whose dude ranch is a fancy version of a boardinghouse, has had her own marriage end "in a towering rage in Reno," leaving her a "virile" woman "who addressed all humankind and all horseflesh in the same way without regard to age or sex. . . ."[55]

"The Ordeal of Conrad Pardee" (1964), in contrast to the stories discussed above, is a whimsical treatment on the theme of the domineering older woman. It concerns the ticklish social problem of a

New York socialite who wishes to be accepted by Mrs. James Grant Grace, a Boston Brahmin, who wields an iron rule over society in the New Hampshire town where Conrad Pardee has his summer home. After outwitting her so that she agrees to come to a party at his home, he—always appropriate, always suave—fumbles his response to her call announcing that she will not after all be able to attend. In a variation upon a line that has charmed all others who have telephoned their regrets, Pardee commits a Freudian slip when he says to Mrs. Grace: "Oh, sad tidings, but do be assured that while we'll be inconvenienced, we'll in no way be heartbroken." After a lengthy silence, Mrs. Grace responds: " 'Well!' she said. 'Well, Mr. Pardee, there you are,' " thereby summing up all her notions of his parvenu New York City origins.[56]

In a similar humorous vein, "A Reasonable Facsimile" (1957) relates the story of a famous professor emeritus's unwanted disciple. When Henry Medley instigates a correspondence with Dr. Bohrmann, the professor is enchanted with the "princely lad." And when the twenty-four-year-old orphan arrives for a visit at his own invitation, Dr. Bohrmann finds him "respectful, responsive, articulate, enthusiastic, astoundingly catholic in his information."[57] He lacks, however, an essential quality; he is unable to express any aspirations or feelings of his own. He is "so unself-centered that Dr. Bohrmann began to wonder if he had a self at all" (*BC,* 76). The professor's concern is confirmed by Medley's becoming the "most sedulous of apes" during his three-week visit. He appropriates Dr. Bohrmann's manner of dress, as well as his politics, his tastes in food and music, even his conversation. The professor's attitude toward the young man moves from boredom to detestation, his first such response to anyone in his life. The professor is finally rescued when Medley asks him to get rid of his cat, to which Medley is terribly allergic. Dr. Bohrmann chooses the cat and Medley must leave.

Stafford says of this story that she was reading the Holmes-Laski correspondence and found there the "kernel" for the story. Nonetheless, she writes: "I cannot tell you how many people have been positively identified as my wholly fictitious Holmes and Laski."[58] No doubt Stafford found the kernel where she indicated, but it is also quite likely that many people assumed, and probably correctly, that Stafford built much of her characterization of Medley from her knowledge of the youthful Robert Lowell, who, at his own invitation, tented out on the lawn of his self-identified mentor Allen Tate for two months during the summer that Stafford first met him. It also seems likely that she included the story in the collection called *Bad Characters* as a subtle stab at her former husband.

In "The Maiden" (1950), a much darker manipulation occurs to Evan Leckie, an unusual figure in Stafford's list of characters. Leckie, an American journalist covering the war crimes trials in Germany, is treated to the grotesque story of the engagement and marriage of the only German couple at a dinner party in Heidelberg. With Leckie and the others held a captive audience, Herr Reinmuth triumphs over the American captors, who grace their tables with the gorgeous contraband resulting from Germany's defeat, by relating how he asked his wife to marry him immediately after he had just witnessed the death by guillotine of his first client. In the telling of the tale, the Reinmuths "had joyfully danced a *Totentanz,* had implied all the details of their sixty-pfennig marriage, and as if there had never been anything untoward in their lives" (*CS,* 55–64).

With the exception of "Mountain Jim," which is examined in chapter 2, the eight stories discussed above are the only ones in Stafford's canon that have males as their central characters, although Ralph in *The Mountain Lion* and Andrew in *The Catherine Wheel* share the central focus with Molly and Katherine. It is noteworthy that five of these stories do not appear in any of the collections of Stafford's stories, and only two appear in *The Collected Stories.* Their absence from the collections emphasizes Stafford's primary concern with female characters.

The organization of the following chapters will follow the ages of woman to which Stafford turned most of her attention. The novels and stories will be discussed not according to their chronological dates of publication, although the dates will be provided, but as they are appropriate to the following thematic divisions: childhood and adolescence, young womanhood, maturity and old age.

Chapter Two
Childhood and Adolescence

Jean Stafford's childhood in the West was a particularly potent influence on her creativity. In the author's note to *The Collected Stories,* she writes: "I have been back to the West, since [first leaving it], only for short periods of time, but my roots remain in the semi-fictitious town of Adams, Colorado, although the rest of me may abide in the South or the Midwest or New England or New York." *The Mountain Lion* and all but one of the stories that portray the lives of young girls are set in the West, most of them in Adams, Stafford's name for Boulder, Colorado. In these works she makes vigorous use of the vernacular of the West and of her experience in the West as a child.

In an essay entitled "Wordman, Spare That Tree," Stafford relates an anecdote that she says she often used to illustrate "the kind of speech I was privileged to hear when I was growing up . . .":

One time when I was out in Colorado visiting my sister, whose husband was a cattle rancher, I was sitting in the kitchen, drinking coffee late in the morning of a hot August day. I was occupied with nothing but coffee drinking and staring into space, a time-consuming but essential exercise for writers. A neighboring rancher had quartered some of his stock on my brother-in-law's range, and he had gone up that morning to cut a bull calf out of the herd to be butchered. He came down to the house for a glass of water, wearing, as he always did, a black hat like a Texas sheriff's, and, as he always did, packing his six-shooter lest he be ambushed by a sheepman. He said to me, "Well, Miss Jean, you still writing books?" I replied that I supposed I was, and he said, "That's a mighty nice kind of job. You can do it in the shade." Then, after a moment's reflection, he said, "But I suppose it must be kinda hard to make the lines come out even."[1]

The Stories

Stafford's ear for Western speech and its appropriation by children is especially evident in the four stories featuring Emily Vanderpool. Two of these, "The Violet Rock" (1952) and "The Scarlet Letter" (1959), are uncollected. One of the other two, "Bad Characters"

(1954), is the title story of Stafford's first collection, which also contains the fourth, "A Reading Problem" (1956). The Emily Vanderpool stories are set in Adams, a kinder place in these stories than it is for other young girls in other stories Stafford sets there. In the author's note to *Bad Characters,* Stafford indicates the autobiographical basis for Emily's personality: "Emily Vanderpool . . . who acknowledges that she has a bad character, is someone I knew well as a child; indeed, I often occupied her skin and, looking back, I think that while she was notional and stubborn and a trial to her kin, her talent for iniquity was feeble—she wanted to be a road-agent but she hadn't a chance. Her troubles stemmed from the low company she kept, but she did not seek these parties out: they found her. It is a wide-spread human experience."

Stafford introduces twelve-year-old Emily in "The Violet Rock," which is narrated by Emily's eight-year-old sister, Tess. On the occasion of going to the foothills to look for pasque flowers, an activity that Stafford often enjoyed as a child, Emily plays on Tess's general fearfulness and terrorizes her into believing that a curse has been placed on her by a wealthy dude. Tess half expects what she gets from the "volatile and clever" Emily. She describes the "bad character" that Emily laments elsewhere. As Emily's frustration over not finding the pasque flowers grows, she builds toward a temper tantrum, a result of "the fury that had bedevilled her" since birth. In the midst of a tantrum, "she would do a kind of writhing witch dance, shrieking out the most appalling imprecations against everyone she had ever known or heard about. . . . Sometimes, when the rage was spent, she turned grayly pale, and not infrequently she vomited and had to be put to bed in a dark room with a wet washrag over her feverish and aching head."[2]

This day in the midst of her rage, "her long, skinny arms were flailing in their blue serge middy-blouse sleeves, her pigtails thrashed, her feet stomped out a warpath . . . , and her mouth was a livid cave from which spewed out, like rats and reptiles, the declarations of her hatred of everyone. . . ." Silhouetted against the sky as she was, Emily appeared to Tess "like some huge injured bird of prey, a little fictitious and a little farcical but exciting and resplendent."[3] It is an understatement to remark that Emily, born to such rages, is an unhappy child.

When Emily tells her own story as an eleven-year-old in "Bad Characters," she is contrite. As a result of just such a rage as her sister describes, she is bereft at the moment of any friends. She has just called Virgil Meade "a son of a sea cook, said it was common knowledge that his mother had bedbugs and that his father, a dentist and the deputy marshall, was a bootlegger on the side" (*CS*, 264). In this position, she encounters Lottie Jump, a hardened eleven-year-old criminal, whom Emily surprises in the theft of a cake from the Vanderpool home.

It is Lottie's "gaudy, cynical talk" that first captivates Emily. She calls Adams "a slow poke town, . . . a one-horse burg" and calls Emily herself, "kid." She makes Emily "think of one of those self-contained dogs whose home is where his handout is and who travels alone but, if it suits him to, will become the leader of a pack" (*CS*, 268). When Emily does not understand Lottie's use of the term *lift*, Lottie replies, "*Steal*, for crying in the beer," and retorts "Ish ka bibble!" when Emily cautions that stealing is a sin and a crime. Despite her misgivings, Emily agrees to join Lottie in a shoplifting spree: "[In] our short meeting she had mesmerized me; I would think about her style of talking and the expert way she had made off with the perfume flask and the cake . . . and be bowled over, for the part of me that did not love God was a black-hearted villain" (*CS*, 274). Besides, she fears that Lottie will avenge any disloyalty. In the end, it is Emily, not Lottie, who is punished for their crime.

Emily encounters similar unsavory characters in "A Reading Problem." Forced by circumstances into leaving the jail—her favorite reading spot, where her friend Sheriff Starbird reads Sax Rohmer's Fu Manchu novels[4]—Emily walks to a camp on the outskirts of town where she is apprehended and threatened by Evangelist Gerlash and his daughter Opal. Stafford displays her love for the western vernacular in the following exchange in which the father and daughter try to blackmail Emily into getting some food for them:

"Whyn't you go get us some eats?" said Opal, cajoling. "If you get us some eats, we won't come calling. If we come calling, like as not we'll spend the night."

"Haven't slept in a bed since May," said her father snuffling.

"We don't shake easy," said Opal, with an absolutely shameless grin. (*CS*, 340)

Underlying the comedy of this situation is the reality that Emily is unable to escape from a pair of fairly rough customers. She is rescued when her friend the sheriff arrives to run the Gerlashes out of town for bootlegging, the profitable sideline of their evangelistic campaign.

"The Scarlet Letter," the slightest of the Emily Vanderpool stories, notable primarily for the slangy language of the children involved, evolves around a plot concocted by Emily and Virgil Meade to protest the amount of geography homework they are assigned to do. After Virgil has cajoled her into sewing her reading achievement letter on her sock rather than where it should be, he deserts her when she presents the petition against the geography assignments to their teacher. Emily is left to get a "sober lecture on the value of geography and the sin of insubordination, the inadvisability of carrying arms, the folly of arrogating power, the extreme impropriety of wearing an honor badge on the leg," delivered by the school principal while he chokes back his laughter at the hilarity of the situation.[5]

The Emily Vanderpool stories, while often comically humorous, nonetheless present a portrait of a young girl who is as tormented by her own uncontrollable rages as are the people around her. Emily says, "My badness never gave me half the enjoyment Jack and Stella thought it did. A good deal of the time I wanted to eat lye" (CS, 274). This self-destructive desire is shared by other girls in Adams less fortunate socially and economically than Emily. An idealized version of Stafford's own family, Emily's family is solidly middle class; her father, who runs the local Safeway store, and her mother are both alive. She has an older and a younger sister and an older brother, who lead the ordinary lives of middle-class children, attending Scouts and taking ballet lessons as a matter of course.

The other young girls in Stafford's Adams stories are orphans, some with a single remaining parent, others with no parent at all. They do their best to accommodate themselves to their situations, but usually lead cramped and painful lives, separated both by time and by sex from the expansive western tradition that is the heritage of the area where they live. The remnants of that tradition linger in the grotesque collection of artifacts that Emily Vanderpool sees in the hotel lobby: "a rusted, beat-up placer pan with samples of ore in it, some fossils and some arrowheads, a tomahawk, a powder horn, and the shellacked tail of a beaver that was supposed to have been trapped by a desperado named Mountain Jim Nugent, who had lived in Estes Park in the seventies" (CS, 325). These "seedy" souvenirs merely point to the heroic, mythic West that was, a West that the young girls get only occasional glimpses of in modern Adams.

For nine-year-old Jessie, "The Healthiest Girl in Town" (1951), Adams is a place of sickness. Her mother, a practical nurse, has brought Jessie there because she is sure to get enough work among the tuberculars to be able to feed and clothe herself and her daughter. Unlike her contemporaries, Jessie cannot take for granted "all the sickness and dying" that they live among: "I did not get used to these people who carried the badge of doom in their pink cheeks as a blind man carries his white stick in his hand" (*CS*, 197). Stafford re-creates in Jessie the same "awful, embarrassed pity" she had felt herself when she met little groups of tuberculars walking in the foothills around Boulder and the same guilt she had felt because her own lungs were healthy.[6]

Jessie was alone with her own father when he died of gangrene. She had stood silently, "blissful with terror," awaiting her mother's return to the hospital room. When Jessie is forced to be friends with the children of a tubercular family in order that her mother's job with the family will remain secure, she is so taunted by the sickly Butler girls that she begins to be ashamed of her own good health. To impress the Butlers, one day she tells them her father died of leprosy. But when she realizes she has been found out, she exultantly shouts: "He got shot out hunting. . . . My father was as tall as this room. The district nurse told Ma that I am the healthiest girl in town. Also I have the best teeth" (*CS*, 216). After thus defying them with her own vitality, she is no longer tortured by the Butler's self-congratulatory attitude toward their own ailments. She must, nevertheless, remain their companion on command or risk the possibility of her mother's losing her job and Jessie's thereby losing the most important thing in the world to her—her Saturday afternoon dancing lessons.

The limitation on their freedom is a fact with which the young girls in the Adams stories must comply. The orphans' freedom is especially limited. Early in their lives they have experienced the deep emotional loss caused by the death of a parent and the resulting psychological and physical deprivation. Jessie is "possessed with the facts of dying and of death." Although she retains the consolation of a loving mother, the two of them must please people like the Butlers in order to live. The distortions in the lives of Emily Vanderpool's alter egos are at least partially explained by missing or disabled parents. Opal Gerlash's mother had died a year before Emily encounters her. Lottie Jump's father is slowly dying of tuberculosis.

The deaths of both their parents place the sisters in "In the Zoo"

(1953) in the hands of the paranoiac Mrs. Placer, the widow of a tubercular husband and a boardinghouse keeper. Griefstricken for their parents and with no responsible relatives to offer them comfort, the girls are left to grow up "like worms," in a house "steeped in . . . mists of accusation and hidden plots and double meanings . . ." (CS, 287). The only comfort in their lives is their friendship with a drunkard Irishman who lives near the railroad tracks with a menagerie of animals. Mrs. Placer's greatest triumph over the sisters is turning the gentle dog that Mr. Murphy gives the girls into a killer that destroys one of his beloved capuchins. The sisters cope with their situation by adapting their behavior to the suspicions of Mrs. Placer, living "in a mesh of lies and evasions, baffled and mean, like rats in a maze" (CS, 300).

As adults, they wonder why they had not fled their situation as soon as they were old enough to work. They realize, the narrator concludes, that Mrs. Placer had "held us trapped by our sense of guilt. We were vitiated, and we had no choice but to wait, flaccidly, for her to die" (CS, 301). The sisters as adults feel themselves at last free of the "succubus" who had preyed on them. Their farewell remarks to each other, however, reveal that they have been permanently damaged by the suspicion and hostility toward other people that Mrs. Placer ingrained in them, even to the point of their unconsciously using her favorite phrase, "I had to laugh," to preface their spiteful remarks about the narrator's fellow passengers.

The horror of the girls' situation in "In the Zoo" is unrelieved by the humor to be found in other Adams stories. In this story, even more than in the ones in which Emily and Jessie appear, the image of the young girl in the West that emerges is that of a human being who is powerless, who has few defenses, who exhibits some degree of self-hatred, who lives in a confined psychological and physical space, and whose actions are restricted to surviving in that space, rather than redefining it. When Stafford fled the West, she was no doubt pursued by the smothering image that she presents in the Adams stories.

"In the Zoo" contains some of those "seeds of truth" from Stafford's life that indicate that the story has some autobiographical basis. The two sisters remember their lives with Mrs. Placer while sitting before the blind polar bear that actually once lived in the Denver Zoo. The sisters' situation parallels the real-life situation of Stafford and one of her sisters. The narrator, as Stafford did, has been on a visit to her sister, who lives as Stafford's sister did, across the Rockies from Denver in western Colorado. The sister has come to Denver with the narrator to see her off on her train east, as it is likely Stafford's own sister had done. It is also likely that Stafford and her sister on such an occasion would have reminisced about their lives growing up in a boardinghouse run by their own mother. Given this revelatory "seed," Stafford's transformation of real life to art in the story reveals how deep ran the resentment and hatred of the real life she had led as the daughter of a boardinghouse keeper. One can speculate that she felt in her misery that she might as well have been an orphan. How much of her own feelings about her mother went into the portrait of Mrs. Placer—and of all the other landladies and boardinghouse keepers she painted so vilely—is impossible to evaluate, for Stafford wrote no nonfictional portrait of her mother.

One of the western stories not set in Adams, "Old Flaming Youth" (1950), is a remarkably good story that was never collected. In it one hears strong echoes of the Twainian influence that Stafford has acknowledged. The story is narrated by Sue Thomas, who is not yet sixteen. She and her younger sister Janie live with their mother and stepfather, Mr. Pendleton, in an unnamed western town. The girls' father had been killed accidentally several years before. To ease their way between the boredom of school days and the evenings during which Mr. Pendleton rants and rages at the dinner table, the girls habitually stop after school to visit the Ferguson twins, who are flashily dressed and slangily spoken high school dropouts with bad reputations. The twins hold the same fascination for the Thomas girls that Lottie Jump holds for Emily Vanderpool. But whereas the result of her escapade with Lottie is primarily hurt pride for Emily, the result of Sue's association with the Ferguson twins is a painful recognition of human callousness, greed, and deception.

The Ferguson twins are also fatherless, living with their mother and her father. The elderly man is generally confined to his rocking chair, speaking unintelligibly to himself. When boys come to visit the twins, some of them carry the old man in his chair to the back porch. Sue's response to the twins' treatment of their grandfather is an echo of the pain in Huck Finn's voice when he views similar inhumanity: "I hated it when they did that because he would look so horribly scared and hang onto the chair arms for dear life and bleat the way Carrie does when I am taking a thorn out of her paw." The twins tell her that he does not care, "that he was really not all there

and anyhow he hadn't any right to mind since he was totally depen-
dent on them and didn't have a red cent to call his own."[7]

Sue discovers the excruciating extension of this attitude one day as
she searches the Fergusons' house for a bracelet they have stolen from
Janie. She finds the grandfather sitting on the front porch, dressed in
absurd, discarded clothing, waiting to be taken away to the County
Home. She also finds out that he can indeed talk and remarks, again
echoing Huck, "It gave me a queer feeling to know that all this time
he had heard the dreadful things his granddaughters had been saying
about him."[8] When she learns that the twins have deliberately left
him to wait alone to be carried away and that his leaving is a result
of the twins' having forced their mother to choose between him and
them, the painfulness of the experience causes Sue to conclude: "I'll
never forget that afternoon as long as I live. . . ."[9]

The first of the western stories Stafford published is "The Darkening Moon" (1944). It is discussed here—almost as summary—because it is emblematic of Stafford's portrayal of the young girl in the
West. Ella, the central character, is eleven years old. Her father has
been dead for one year. She lives in a small, nameless mining town.
Her story takes place completely at night. When we first see her, she
is "alone beneath the black firmament and between the blacker
mountains that [loom] up to the right and to the left of her like the
blurred figures of fantastic beasts" (CS, 252). She makes a trip she
often makes, riding her brother's horse several miles through the dark
to babysit at an isolated farm on the other side of the town. Sometimes she dreads the trip because the horse tries to throw her if it is
frightened by the high bluffs along the highway. Tonight she has the
added danger of carrying through town ten pounds of elk meat her
brother has poached.

Ella postpones her arrival at the farm as long as she dares, knowing
that this will be like all the other evenings she has spent there:
"Afraid to move lest by moving she make a noise that would obscure
another noise . . . , she would sit motionless all evening in a big
pink wing chair. . . . By midnight she would be wringing wet with
sweat, although it was cold and she had let the fire go out. And yet,
as soon as she had mounted for the ride back, her fear had changed
its focus and she was not anxious to get home, but only to get Squaw
safely past the bluff" (CS, 254). This night is like the others, except
that Ella endures the additional horror of a total eclipse of the moon.

Stripped of its narrative particulars, this story embodies Stafford's
version of the mythic journey possible to young girls in the West.

An orphaned child travels through a dark landscape riding a steed that she has difficulty controlling because the landscape itself threatens the beast. Her destination is a place where she sits paralyzed by fear. She is released from her place of paralysis only to travel once again through the threatening landscape and to return to where she began. This is not the triumphant journey of a hero. Her dark night of the soul does not release her finally into the light of new perceptions and new possibilities. Instead, it is a journey that she is doomed to repeat. The repetition and the willingness with which the young girl reenters her paralysis distinguishes the horror of her situation. She has accepted the journey as normality.

In one of the last stories she published, Stafford shows how differently she sees the possibilities for a young boy in a very similar situation. In "Mountain Jim" (1968), twelve-year-old Tim Talbot is left alone one night at the isolated Kavanagh ranch, high in a valley of the Colorado Rockies. Tim, busily working a jigsaw puzzle, does not notice the kinds of sounds that freeze Ella to her chair. He does notice when all the noises cease to a "deathly quiet." Tim's response is to go to the back porch for root beer, where he is reassured by the sights and smells of the outdoors. When the moon is briefly covered by a dense cloud, however, he hears a dog yelp and a horse neigh "crazily" and he hears a man's voice.

As the moonlight returns, he sees, as Ella does, "horses running in wild confusion, rearing up on their hind legs, pawing the earth with their forefeet, snorting and nickering."[10] He also sees the man and the dog dodging among the horses, apparently walking through the high wire fence, and disappearing in the direction of the potato cellar. Tim returns inside the house, but not to stay there locked in fear. He reasons that there is a clear explanation for everything he has seen and heard. Finally, however, he decides he must determine for himself how the man and the dog got through the fence.

He takes his .22 rifle and his dog and goes to find out. He finds no sign on the fence of the passage of the two. At the potato cellar, he gets a strong sense of the presence of the man inside, even though the cellar is strongly padlocked. Tim knows that the "sensible" action would be to return to the ranchhouse, but he will not be "cheated out of an adventure." When the man and the dog do in fact emerge from the cellar, Tim not only stands his ground; he moves even nearer to the apparition before him, for although his "fear was great, . . . his curiosity was greater."[11] After an exchange in which the man identifies himself as Mountain Jim Nugent, the man and dog disappear in thin air. Tim calmly returns to the house and to his puzzle.

Tim Talbot had encountered the ghost of a famous nineteenth-century mountain man, the same Mountain Jim Nugent mentioned in "A Reading Problem." In real life, Nugent had been befriended by Isabella L. Bird, author of *A Lady's Life in the Rocky Mountains,* one of Stafford's favorite old books. Stafford told Dick Cavett that she and a friend at the University of Colorado had actually located the site of Mountain Jim's cabin. [12]

Tim's night alone stands in stark contrast to Ella's. The sights and sounds of Ella's night reduce her to passivity and fear. The same kind of situation spurs Tim to action, equipped with the manly trappings of a rifle and a large dog. The result for Tim is an increased sense of self-assuredness. One may conclude from these two stories that Stafford viewed even the modern West as a very different place for boys than it is for girls, a view she elaborates specifically in *The Mountain Lion.*

"Cops and Robbers" (1953) is the one story Stafford wrote about a child that is not set in the West. Five-year-old Hannah becomes a pawn in the deadly marital game being played out by her fashionable eastern parents. Her "spun gold" hair is her mother's delight, reflecting as it does her own hair. The two are having a portrait painted in which their beautiful hair is accented. In the midst of the sittings and following a particularly vicious fight between her parents, Hannah's father takes her to a barber shop and has her hair cut in a boy's short style. Hannah, four days after being shorn, sits hidden on the attic stairs in abject misery, powerless either to understand or to overcome her situation:

> It was ugly and ungenerous here where she was, on the narrow, splintery stairs, and up in the attic a mouse or a rat scampered on lightly clicking claws between the trunks. . . . Something like sleep touched her eyeballs. . . . But it was tears, not drowsiness that came. They fell without any help from her; . . . no part of her body was affected at all except the eyes themselves, from which streamed down these mothering runnels. (*CS*, 424)

The horror of the situation is that in the conversation Hannah overhears from her hiding place, her mother expresses little concern over the painful experience Hannah is enduring. Instead, she is absorbed in the pain her husband's action has caused her and the fury she feels at her husband for ruining the portrait—which would have been a reflection of her own beauty. The mother reveals herself, at last, as insensitive to her own small daughter as is Mrs. Placer to her foster children in "In the Zoo."[13]

The Mountain Lion

The Mountain Lion, the best of Stafford's novels, records four years in the lives of Ralph and Molly Fawcett, ending with Molly's death at thirteen from a rifle shot fired by Ralph, two years her senior. In the course of the four years, the children, whose father had died before Molly was born, transfer their loyalties, which were never very strong, from their mother and two older sisters and life in Covina, California, to life as it is lived on the Colorado ranch of their Uncle Claude, their mother's half-brother and the son of their beloved Grandpa Kenyon, who dies early in the novel on his annual visit to Covina.

Ralph and Molly are misfits in their own family. Their mother and their beautiful sisters are completely at home with the "Eastern" values that Mrs. Fawcett has transported to Covina from St. Louis and which provide a superficial patina on their lives there. Mrs. Fawcett is embarrassed by her stepfather Kenyon and has, instead, made her living room a monument to her own father, the children's Grandfather Bonney, a merchant in Missouri, who had been born in Boston. Beneath his portrait "on the mantle which was black marble and had been taken from the house in St. Louis, stood [his] christening cup and the Florentine urn which held his ashes."[14] On this altar stood other mementos—a silver snuff box, a miniature Venus de Milo, a gold stamp box, and a jewel case containing the trinkets that Ralph, Grandfather Bonney's namesake, would eventually inherit.

Everything about Grandpa Kenyon, on the other hand, dismays Mrs. Fawcett and the older girls—"his table manners, his rough and ungrammatical speech, his clothes, and his profession" (18)—despite the fact that his four cattle ranches have made him a multimillionaire. By contrast, Ralph and Molly are enchanted by Grandpa Kenyon and chafe under the forced gentility of occasions like the visits by the Reverend Follansbee and his wife, which become paeans to their Grandfather Bonney's life. Stafford based her description of Kenyon on her own paternal grandfather, and her own fondness for the character as well as her ear for the language of the West is demonstrated in the speech with which she helps to characterize Kenyon.

When the children take him to see a dry wash near their house in Covina, he responds, " 'Well, now, that's something like it. There's too damn much green in this here California. But that dried-up little old crick bed down there makes me think of a place that *is* a place.' He swept his black eyes round the scene and breathed shallowly as if the sweetness of the orange blossoms offended him and he said, 'To think there ain't any winter here! Why, I'd as lief go to hell in a handbasket as not to see the first snow fly' " (7).

Ralph and Molly's emotional distance from their mother and their sisters is further captured in the difference of their physical selves from the others. As eight- and ten-year-olds, Molly and Ralph are physically ugly. A bout of scarlet fever lingers with them as a glandular disorder causing frequent bad nosebleeds. They are "thin, pallid, and runny-nosed. From some obscure ancestor they had inherited bad, uneven teeth and nearsighted eyes so that they had to wear braces and spectacles. Their skin and hair and eyes were dark and the truth of it was they always looked a little dirty. They were small for their age but they had large bones . . ." (28). In their ugliness and in their precocity, they are friendless, except for each other.

Ralph wishes to escape California and "go out West" to Colorado, because both he and Molly accept Grandpa Kenyon's observation that "California was not the West but was a separate thing like Florida and Washington, D.C." (8). This wish is finally realized after Grandpa Kenyon's death. When Molly and Ralph arrive at the ranch, however, they find that "the landscape itself was frightening. Above timberline the snow was thick in the deep gashes; to the north were two long glaciers which sometimes shone pink through the haze. . . . Below timberline and above the dry sagebrush of the foothills, the forests of conifers were dense . . . here and there interrupted by a small grove of golden aspens or a bright upland meadow. . . . The mountains were at once remote . . . and oppressively confining. . . . [They] wore peril conspicuously on their horny faces" (95). Against this frightening and quintessentially Western landscape, Ralph and Molly begin their transition from childhood to adolescence, a transition that takes them down separate paths, destroys their childhood intimacy, and reenacts, as Blanche Gelfant has pointed out, the classic American myth of growth to manhood, with its resultant tragedies.[15]

Events that take place their first summer at the ranch cause an estrangement between Molly and Ralph, so that for subsequent summers there "they all but ignored one another," although in Covina they remain close, in opposition to the others. The first event occurs on a day that the two go mountain climbing with Claude and Winifred, the housekeeper's daughter, the day that Ralph later remembers as "the day his friendship with Uncle Claude had begun and the day on which he had abandoned Molly" (223). On that day, Claude asks Ralph why he does not quit wearing his glasses. Ralph does quit. This step begins the breach between him and Molly, because, although she tries, Molly cannot abandon hers. It is Ralph's first step away from his childhood ugliness and weakness, but Molly's near blindness prevents her from following him.

The second event is Ralph's watching a cow give birth. He accepts this occurrence without embarrassment, but with wonder. When he tries to tell Molly about his first experience with the realities of sexuality, Molly rebels at the notion, calls him a "dirty liar," and brings on a nosebleed. Ralph's accommodation to the event takes him one step further from Molly. He can, as a result, accept with some equanimity the belief that Uncle Claude visits prostitutes in the nearby town. Molly, on the other hand, denies sexuality to the point of deliberately misunderstanding the concept of marriage. She wants to marry a horse during the first summer at the ranch. She once declared she was engaged to a dog. Even at twelve, she insists that she and Ralph will marry and stay in Covina rather than go to Connecticut when Mrs. Fawcett sells the house and moves there.

While Molly clings to the safety (and ugliness) of her childhood, Ralph has begun to feel the result of Grandpa Kenyon's desire that they be sent to Colorado so that Ralph can learn "the ways of a man." He starts that learning, and as the years pass his childhood awkwardness begins to disappear. By the time he is fourteen, he has begun to fill out: "he had lost his pallor and his eyes, quite strong, were clear." In contrast, Molly retains "her ugly face and her lankiness and the slouching, round-shouldered gait which she had developed and which caused her enemies to call her 'the crab' " (128).

During the winter before they return to the ranch for their final year-long stay—while Mrs. Fawcett tours the world with their sisters—Ralph decides "that the world was made up of two groups of people. The first he called 'Kenyon men' and this included those who, like Uncle Claude, knew the habits of animals and subjected themselves to the government of the seasons. The other group he called 'Bonney merchants' and this included everyone he had ever

known" with the exception of the people at the Bar K, Grandpa, and
Molly" (114). In returning to the ranch, Ralph intends to become
one of the "Kenyon men."

Molly, however, remains on a course that isolates her further and
further from everybody, including Ralph. The train trip from Denver
to the ranch decides their directions. During the trip, Ralph fights
against incestuous thoughts of his sister Leah, finally turning mutely
to Molly as his salvation; she alone did not "urge him to corruption."
He destroys that safehold, however, by whispering to her as the train
travels through the darkness of a tunnel, "Molly, tell me all the dirty
words you know" (158). Although Molly is too startled to respond,
"Ralph's childhood and his sister's expired at that moment of the
train's entrance into the surcharged valley. It was a paradox, for now
they should be going into a tunnel with no end, now that they had
heard the devil speak" (159).

As emotionally close as Ralph and Molly have been as children—
almost two sides of the same coin—Molly's strangeness and posses-
siveness trouble Ralph increasingly as they grow older. In his tenth
year, he expresses his reservations about her in a way that signals his
own sense of superiority. He does not like the way she copies him,
although he finds it "natural" that she would like to be a boy. He
scolds her for wearing his Boy Scout shirt, saying, "Having that on
a girl is like dragging the American flag in the dirt" (30). When he
is baffled by Molly's poem "Gravel" and by a letter she writes, he
expresses his view to his Uncle Claude that Molly is crazy. At the
ranch the first summer, Ralph softens this view and decides that
Molly is "just different from other people. . . . He liked her when
they were alone, but she embarrassed him in public because she said
such peculiar things" (94). But when Molly looks at him with "her
large humble eyes fondling his face with lonely love, he wanted to
cry out with despair because hers was really the only love he had and
he found it nothing but a trial and tribulation" (116).

By the time Ralph is fourteen, his perplexity with Molly makes
him wish "oftener and oftener that she did not exist" (128). Molly,
in her isolation and estrangement from him, shares his wish. In the
closing days of their last year in Covina, Molly expresses her own self-
hatred, saying to Ralph, "in a cold, level voice, 'I know I'm ugly. I
know everybody hates me. I wish I were dead' " (139). She knows
her appearance justifies her statement, because not only is she ugly,
but she has "a homemade look, a look of having been put together

by an inexperienced hand" (140). Ralph finally wishes Molly "had
never been born" (144).

Molly's strangeness takes on a darker coloration during their final
year at the Bar K. On their first evening there, Uncle Claude warns
her: "If you don't watch out, they're going to put you in the booby
hatch. I never seen anybody in my life with such damn crazy ideas"
(164). In her fierce denial of sexuality, Molly performs a bathtub ritual that is designed to prevent herself and everyone else from seeing
her body. She, in fact, avoids even using the word *body* and is horri-
fied when anyone else does. Instead, she "thought of herself as a long
wooden box with a mind inside" (177). As a record of her isolation,
Molly keeps a list of unforgivable people. The only two people she
finds completely forgivable are her father and Grandpa Kenyon. This
year, walking in the mountains, she feels as if she "had been by herself" since Kenyon's death. Lying in the tub that first evening, reflecting on her new hatred of Ralph, she decides to add his name to
the list, which already includes Grandfather Bonney, her mother and
sisters, the Follanbees, and various former friends. By Christmas, she
has added Winifred's and Claude's names. And, finally, in an act that
echoes her earlier wish that she were dead, she adds her own.

While Molly's rejection of the people who form her world thus
progresses, Ralph's identification with those people, and particularly
with Claude, intensifies. On the same evening on which Molly ritu-
ally purifies herself, Ralph embarks fully on that journey to manhood, foreseen by Grandpa Kenyon, that is made possible by his
having gone "out West." Claude shows Ralph a bull with a hairball
in his jaw, rolling in pain in a small pasture near the ranchhouse. As
the man and the boy watch in "brutal preoccupation, their companionship was so complete that it almost frightened Ralph; it was as
though he had set forth on an adventure whose terms were so inex-
orable that he could not possibly change his mind and go back, as if
they were on a boat in the middle of a landless sea" (167–68). The
adventure on which Ralph sets out with his uncle is figuratively the
search for his manhood. Literally, from this evening, the adventure
is a hunt for a mountain lion Claude has named Goldlilocks, and the
hunt is one he refuses to share with anyone but Ralph.

The mountain lion has formed a leitmotiv in Ralph and Claude's
relationship from the time of Claude's trip to Covina for Grandpa
Kenyon's funeral, when Claude tells Ralph he has never seen one. At
the end of their first summer on the ranch, Claude again tells Ralph

he has never seen one. Ralph's fantasy of killing a mountain lion begins that day: "He wished he would be hiking by himself in the
mountains one day and suddenly come on a lion's den. He would
shoot the mother and the cubs and then take Uncle Claude up to see.
He could just hear Uncle Claude suck in his breath and say, 'Well,
I'll be a son-of-a-gun' " (113). The competitive desire to prove his
manhood that this fantasy incorporates continues four years later
when Ralph learns that Claude has finally sighted a lion. Ralph remains "enraptured" with the thought of the lion while he and Claude
fruitlessly search for her.

As the year develops, Ralph grows ambivalent about his relationship to Claude, caused in part by his troubled state of mind about his
own growing sexuality. He nonetheless remains absorbed with the
idea of killing the mountain lion and determines that it will be he,
and not Claude, who succeeds in the hunt. After their first sighting
of the lion, Ralph dreams of her and thinks, " 'Oh, if I don't get her,
I will die!' . . . [He] wanted her because he loved her, but Uncle
Claude wanted her only because she was something rare. Besides,
Uncle Claude would be here forever and could get another, but this
was Ralph's last chance" (218). Ralph's urgency to succeed at this
"last chance" emphasizes his subconscious awareness that this act will
fulfill his Grandpa Kenyon's prophecy and he will become the man
he wishes to be. Their sighting of the lion at Christmas and at Easter
underscores the ritual nature that the hunt has taken on for Ralph.

On Garland Peak, where Ralph's friendship with Claude had begun on a similar late day in spring, he completes his identification
with Claude's manhood and he finally rids himself forever of Molly.
In the glade that Molly had considered her private study, the place
where she had gone all fall and winter to escape from the others and
to do her writing, Ralph sights Goldilocks, the lion. Without waiting for Claude, he fires his rifle, only to be stunned by Claude's shot
from another direction a split second later. When they enter the
glade, it is clear that it is Claude's shot that has downed the lion.
Equally clear, it is Ralph's that has pierced Molly's forehead, where
it has found her on her way to "her" glade. After the Christmas
sighting, Molly had been afraid and she felt she would not feel safe
in the mountains again until the lion had been shot. Finally, it is
Ralph who is safe. In attempting to kill the lion, he has symbolically
killed his childhood by actually killing the person who is a constant
reminder to him of his lost innocence.

Molly's death is the inevitable conclusion for a young girl in the West who cannot accept the limited "normality" possible to her. She is unable to join the feminine world of her mother and her sisters, with its emphasis on female beauty, superficial feelings, charming games, and the pursuit of "beaux." Her mother, in fact, sees to it that Molly is excluded, is sent to Colorado, while Leah and Rachel are sent to Eastern finishing schools and finally are presented to "society" on a world tour. Molly is prevented from entering this world not only because she is not pretty, but also because she has a tough, eccentric mind: "Everyone said that she had the brains of the family, but as Mrs. Fawcett was not interested in brains, she thought this a handicap rather than otherwise and often told Molly that there were other things in life besides books" (143–44).

Molly does use books to fence out what she abhors, both in Covina and in Colorado. Furthermore, she considers writing her vocation and plans to write her own books. At eight she writes "Gravel," the poem that makes Ralph question her sanity:

> Gravel, gravel on the ground
> Lying there so safe and sound,
> Why is it you look so dead?
> Is it because you have no head?

In her last year in Colorado, she writes a long ballad, a short detective novel, and a short story about a leper colony. The poem and the story of the leper colony, which has one character with a "spitcurl of oleaginous hair," reveal both Molly's precociousness and her distaste for close human contact, with its implied sexuality.

Molly's tough, eccentric mind will not accommodate her own sexuality or anyone else's. She wills herself into a state of arrested development, rejecting not only the female model represented by her mother and sisters, but also the model represented by Winifred Brotherman, who changes from a sexually neutral young ranchhand into a very attractive young college woman and thereby becomes "unforgivable" to Molly. Molly cannot participate in the ritual that leads Ralph away from her and their former closeness. Part of Ralph's mission is necessarily to free himself from this entanglement. Molly is left, finally, with no choice that is acceptable to her. When she adds her own name to her list of unforgivable people, she signals her inability to live in the world as it exists for her. She cannot reenter the

"Bonney Bourgeois" world her mother plans for them in Connecticut. She cannot, by definition, become a Kenyon *man* of the western myth. She must, then, die, because she is incapable of making herself fit. There is no place for her—West or East. Unlike her creator, she cannot "hotfoot" it to a place more agreeable to her. No doors are open.

The Mountain Lion has a strong autobiographical basis. The Fawcett family is recognizably based on Stafford's own, with the significant differences that the father is dead and that the family has some money and position. The four children re-create the four Stafford children—the older girls, the younger boy, and the younger girl who is devoted to her brother. The Fawcetts live, as the Staffords did, in Covina, California, in a house with a lippia lawn, next to a walnut grove. The mother is from Missouri, as Mrs. Stafford was. Grandpa Kenyon, like Stafford's paternal grandfather, has cattle ranches in Texas and Missouri (but unlike his prototype also has ranches in Oklahoma and Colorado). One night the Jesse James gang had ridden into his Missouri ranch asking for shelter, just as Stafford's father, in a perhaps apocryphal story, had told her the James gang had come to his father's ranch. Grandfather Bonney is given some of the history of Stafford's maternal grandfather. The scenes in Colorado are re-created from Stafford's own perceptions of the Rocky Mountains when she was a child. Doubtless, the mountain lion was suggested by the real lion Stafford and her college friends had seen in the hills above Boulder.

Most significantly, however, Stafford closely identifies Molly with herself. Molly writes "Gravel" and the stories that Stafford had actually written as a child. She is fiercely devoted to her brother, as Stafford was to hers. She performs the kind of ritual bath that Stafford herself performed as a child from an overwhelming fear of water.[16] Finally, she feels the deep isolation from her family that Stafford apparently felt from her own. Stafford's attachment to the character is apparent in the author's note to the 1972 reissue of the novel: "Poor old Molly. I loved her dearly and I hope she rests in peace."

When Stafford wrote *The Mountain Lion,* her own brother had recently been killed in World War II. One can speculate that in writing the novel she was coming to terms with her feelings about her relationship to her brother. Perhaps in the ending of the novel she was expressing a subconscious wish that it had been he, rather than she, who had survived. To Stafford's fury, only a week before *The*

Mountain Lion was published, Robert Lowell published "Her Dead Brother," which, according to C. David Heymann, "represents a response in part" to the novel. In the poem, the brother is killed and the sister survives. Stressing the theme of latent incest, a theme suggested in the novel, the poem seemed to Stafford "an act so dishonorable that it was almost insane."[17]

Chapter Three
Young Womanhood

Stafford's fiction that develops young women characters reveals her need to address in fictional form some of the most powerful of her own experiences. The autobiographical basis for many of them is quite clear. Stafford has written about the same experiences—but without the dark overtones of the fiction—in essays, where she identifies them as her own. In the corresponding fiction she has often used the same words and phrases in describing incidents that she uses in the essays. The facts of the incidents remain the same, although the fiction supplies the emotional interpretation that is absent in the essays. While Stafford's fiction that portrays children and adolescents often has a snappy humor and wit that can soften—but can also heighten—the ironic and sometimes tragic innocence of childhood, the stories portraying young women, and particularly those that are highly autobiographical, are characterized more frequently by the language of bitterness, fear, anguish, and panic. Most of the young women are isolated and feel trapped—by their poverty, their pain, their inability to control their own destinies.

The Stories

Because most of the stories fit the realities of Stafford's own journey through young womanhood, the discussion that follows is organized around the events in Stafford's life that produced the fiction: her college years at the University of Colorado in Boulder, her student year in Heidelberg, her attempts to find a job after her return, her year teaching at Stephens College, and her early years on the American East Coast.

Two of the three stories set in Adams (Boulder) are specially identifiable as fictional accounts of Stafford's own experiences as a college student there. The dominant images in all three stories, however, are constricting and life-denying. Asked in 1971 about her feelings about the autobiographical Adams stories, Stafford replied: "No, I don't feel bitter, I feel satiric. I felt much bitterer when I was younger, but now I'm mellowing. (pauses) No, that isn't true. I've no way to test myself, because I've retired to a hermit's life. . . ."[1] Perhaps Stafford paused because she remembered that two of the most closely rendered and painful stories of that time had been published a very few years previous to her interview: "The Tea Time of Stouthearted Ladies," in 1964, and "The Philosophy Lesson," in 1968. There is a special clarity and keenness about each of these stories, in which Stafford fictionalized particularly harsh experiences in her own life. Although she had written lightheartedly about her college years in "Souvenirs of Survival" in 1960, these two stories show the grimness for Stafford of working in her mother's boardinghouse and the outrages of her summer job at the dude ranch as well as the physical and psychological pain of modeling for life-drawing classes at the university.

In "The Tea Time of Stouthearted Ladies," Kitty Winstanley lives between her mother's self-delusions about her family's position and Kitty's own harshly realistic perception. Kitty's family—and those of other landladies in Adams—had " 'come down in the world,' but they had descended from a stratum so middling, so snobbish, and so uncertain of itself that it had looked on penury as a disgrace . . ." (*CS*, 221). To compensate, Mrs. Winstanley and her friends have "straitjacketed the life of the town" with "maniacal respectability" (*CS*, 227).

From her bedroom, overhearing her mother and a Mrs. Ewing creating a fantasy of Kitty's summer job at a dude ranch, Kitty visualizes them sitting below in the kitchen in an image that captures both the extreme difficulties of their lives and their careful pretensions: "Their tumid hands mutilated by work would be clasped loosely on the tulip-patterned oilcloth and their swollen feet would be demurely crossed as they glibly evaluated the silver lining of the cloud beneath which they and their families lived, gasping for every breath" (*CS*, 220). Kitty listens "with revulsion, with boredom, pity, outrage . . ." (*CS*, 220). She knows the realities that the women do not dare mention to each other because otherwise they could not bear their shame. Kitty has for years heard the bitter whispers from her parents' bedroom, sometimes lasting all night. As a result, she hates her father for his ineffectualness and her mother for her injustice. Most terribly, however, she hates herself "for hating in them what they could not help" (*CS*, 222).

The landladies console themselves with the social achievements of the well-to-do student boarders and fool themselves with fantasies about the drudgery and embarrassments of the lives of their own children, who were, as Kitty well understood, "exhausted from classes and study and part-time jobs and perpetually starved for status (they loathed the School of Hard Knocks, they hated being Barbarians) and clothes (a good deal of the time they were *not* warm) and fun" (*CS*, 224). Especially humiliating to the sons and daughters was that at home they became maids or footmen to their fellow students who boarded at their mothers' houses.

While Mrs. Winstanley's fantasy about Kitty's summers at the dude ranch is far from the truth of her experience there, Kitty yearns for the time she can return. At the Caribou, she is released from the humiliation of her life at home. As a servant there, she enjoys "a servant's prerogative of keeping her distance . . ." (*CS*, 228). There she knows no one in any other context: "Friendless, silent, long and exasperating, the summers, indeed, were no holiday. But she lived them in pride and without woe . . ." (*CS*, 228). Kitty survives by refusing the hypocrisy that sustains her mother and her friends. She maintains her integrity by looking reality straight in the face and acknowledging the irony that life forces upon her.

"The Philosophy Lesson" is the story that resulted from the several attempts Stafford made to write a novel about the suicide that profoundly affected her when she was a college student. Both she and a very wealthy young woman had been in love with the same young man. The other young woman committed suicide.[2] In the fictionalized account, it is the young man who dies. The description of Cora Savage during the action of "The Philosophy Lesson" is the most constricted image of a young woman, except for Pansy Vanneman in "The Interior Castle," in all of Stafford's fiction. Cora has "turned herself to stone" (*CS*, 362) for the three hours that she poses nude for the life class. She rests only at the end of each of the first two hours. Although in "Souvenirs of Survival" Stafford had called her own modeling at the University of Colorado the "best paying" job on campus and implied her happiness in obtaining it, she omitted the painful details, which she reveals as she describes Cora's situation:

Usually . . . the tension of her muscles would not allow her to think or to pursue a fantasy to a happy ending. . . . Often she felt she must now surely faint or cry out against the pain that began midway through the first hour, began as an itching and a stinging in the part of her body that bore the most weight and then gradually overran her like a disease until the whole configuration of bone and muscle dilated and all her pulses throbbed. Nerves jerked in her neck and a random shudder seized her shoulder blades and sometimes, although it was cold in the studio, all her skin was hot and the blood roared; her heart deafened her. If she had closed her eyes, she would have fallen down. . . . (*CS*, 362)

The modeling is equally painful for Cora emotionally. The art students react to her as they would to inanimate objects for a still life. They talk about her as an object, as if she could not hear. She is "at once enraged and fascinated" by her anonymity (*CS*, 362). When one of the students admiringly asks her if she plans to be a professional model, she is especially dismayed: "the servant whose ambitions go beyond his present status does not wish to be complimented on the way he polishes the silver" (*CS*, 363).

Cora—like Stafford, a philosophy student—escapes only in her mind, by counting to hundreds or, on this day when the snow flies, by the consolation of Bishop Berkeley's philosophy: "she concluded that she would be at peace forever if she could believe that she existed only for herself and possibly for a superior intelligence and that no one existed for her save when he was tangibly present" (*CS*, 365). Both this "quieting phenomenon" and her "inhuman" ability to remain frozen in position are tested when a student bursts into the class to announce the suicide of a young man with whom Cora has been infatuated, although his wealth and his love affair with a wealthy young woman put him out of Cora's social range. Cora holds her pose throughout the ensuing uproar in the classroom. It masks the terror that shakes her as she asks herself what could have driven this privileged young man to his death: "And yet, why not? Why did not she, who was seldom happy, do it herself?" (*CS*, 369). Cora's contemplation of suicide is her ultimate rejection of herself and her entrapping and painful existence.

The third Adams story, "The Liberation" (1953), is not directly autobiographical, as are the two discussed above. It is possible, however, that it was partly inspired by Stafford's marriage at twenty-five to Harvard-educated, Boston-born and -bred Robert Lowell. The heroine, Polly Bay, nearly thirty, orphaned seven years earlier by the death of her father and many years before by her mother's death, has been held an emotional hostage by her father's widowed brother and widowed sister. When she becomes engaged to a professor at Harvard, whom she meets on a visit to Boston, she fully understands for the first time the control that has been exerted upon her. She waits five months to tell her aunt and uncle that she intends to leave Adams and go east to marry, otherwise "she might have had to flee, without baggage, in the middle of the night on a bus" (*CS*, 306). Stafford, of course, had done just that in leaving Iowa on her own flight to Boston.

Polly's emotional oppression is symbolized by the house in which she lives with her aunt and uncle:

Its rooms were huge, but since they were gorged with furniture and with garnishments and clumps and hoards of artifacts of Bays, you had no sense of space in them and, on the contrary, felt cornered and nudged and threatened by hanging lamps with dangerous dependencies and by the dark, bucolic pictures of Polly's forebears that leaned forward from the walls in their unsculptured brassy frames. (*CS*, 308)

This house is on a claustrophobia-inducing city block that had once been home to the entire Bay clan, from Polly's great-grandmother through to her own generation: "[T]his was the territory of the Bays and . . . Bays and ghosts of Bays were, and forever would be in residence" (*CS*, 309). Intent on leaving, Polly finally realizes that in this place "her own life had been like a dream of smothering" (*CS*, 309).

As she confronts her aunt and uncle with her plans, she perceives "appalled and miserably ashamed of herself, that she had never once insisted on her own identity in this house" (*CS*, 310). Her struggle with her aunt and uncle is compounded by their western chauvinism as well as their need to hold on to their family. They reduce her to screaming her hatred of the West and finally to fleeing, as she had fantasized, without baggage and in the night, to the East, to Boston, where her fiancé is now suddenly dead. As she sits in the train, alone, torn from her past and bereft of the future that had been promised her, she surveys her position with unconscious irony: "I am not lonely now" (*CS*, 322).

"The Mountain Day" (1956) was suggested to Stafford by a story told her by Katherine White.[3] It is also set in Colorado but is rather far removed in its outer trappings, although not in its ironic core, from the stories set in Adams. Judy Grayson, the heroine and narrator, has everything Stafford did not have in her own life in Colorado. Judy, a Bryn Mawr undergraduate, only visits the West. She describes her family's position: "Our life was sumptuous and orderly, and we lived it, in the winter, in New York and, in the summer, in the mountains of Colorado. The Grayson fortune, three generations old, [was] founded on such tangibles as cattle, land, and cargo vessels . . ." (*CS*, 222). Judy relates the events of her "storybook summertime romance" with Rod Stephansson, "woven in the mountain sun and mountain moonlight" (*CS*, 234). The "storybook" quality of Judy's view of events allows her such transports as her cry: "Is there anything on earth more unearthly than to be in love at eighteen? It is like an abundant spring garden. My heart was the Orient, and the sun rose from it . . ." (*CS*, 236), language that is markedly different from the pithiness of the speech in most of Stafford's western stories.

Judy is brought up short in her rapture when, on a perfect "mountain day," her grandmother's Irish maids drown in the heart-shaped lake between her father's cabin and her grandmother's house. Not only do the maids drown, but in the few hours they lie in the water, "their lovely faces and their work-swollen hands" are eaten away by the hellbenders and the turtles that live in the lake's deepest holes (*CS*, 247). This tragedy, occurring in the symbolically shaped lake, shakes Judy from the egocentricity of her love affair, and she finds a new definition of love—"wanting the beloved to be happy" (*CS*, 249). The stark image of the mutilated corpses of the young maids is, however, the most powerful in the story. Stafford's choosing to juxtapose it against Judy's charmed life causes a deeper impact than does the happy ending suggested for Judy. The image symbolizes the violence and danger waiting for unprotected "innocent" women in the West.

Of the two stories showing young American women as "innocents abroad"[4] in Europe, one, "The Echo and the Nemesis" (1956), is set in Heidelberg. Sue Ledbetter, one of the central characters, does not appear to be autobiographical, except in the sense that she, like Stafford, is a student at the university and shares some of Stafford's sense of dislocation. The ambience of Heidelberg and the student world there is, of course, drawn from Stafford's experience.

The story is apparently entirely fictional. Stafford has said that the other central character, Ramona Dunn (whose name came from a character in an early version of "A Winter's Tale"),[5] was based on a roommate she once lived with in Cambridge who was a compulsive eater.[6] Stafford also has written that the phrase *adiposa dolorosa*, which she read in a medical textbook, influenced her creation of the character: "I think that 'sorrowful fat' must have stuck in my mind and that the adjective led to my invention of Ramona's despair and her concealing, consoling paranoia."[7] Whatever its origins, "The Echo and the Nemesis" is one of the most profoundly disturbing of Stafford's works. As well as exploring Ramona's psychosis, the story implies that sexual perversion is the basis for it.

Sue and Ramona meet as American students at the University of Heidelberg. Sue, the "innocent," has come directly from America; Ramona, after a childhood in New York, has lived the past ten years with her family in Italy. Sue, whose father is dead, forms a somewhat inadvertent acquaintance with Ramona, because she is "self-conscious and introverted and [does] not make friends easily" (CS, 35). She secretly envies the merrymaking of the other American students at her pension. Ramona, excessively intellectual, scorns those hijinks and spends the coffee hour they share endlessly discoursing on the esoterica of philology. One coffee hour, the radio music at the Konditorei Luitpold suddenly shifts from the usual choruses from *William Tell* to the "Minuet in G," a change that provokes a stream of confidences from Ramona, including a remark that her twin sister, Martha, had been dead for five years. She also suggests "in tantalizing innuendoes" the infidelity of her parents. After detailing her mother's current affair, she seems "on the point of disclosing her father's delinquencies when she [is] checked by a new mood, which [makes] her lower her head, flush," and maintain a long silence (CS, 42).

From this conversation, an intimacy develops on Ramona's part into which Sue is reluctantly drawn. Ramona, who is "fat to the point of parody" (CS, 36), appoints Sue to oversee her agonizing battle with gluttony, which often makes her feel suicidal. Sue watches as Ramona's schizophrenia gradually emerges, in fits of abjectness, paranoia, rage, and in a mixture of lies and evasions about her family, her doctor, her sister Martha. It climaxes when Sue finds inscribed on the back of "Martha's" photograph, "Martha Ramona Dunn at sixteen, Sorrento." She recognizes Ramona's "desperate fabrication" and supposes "in a sense . . . the Martha side of Ramona Dunn *was* dead, dead and buried under layers and layers of fat" (CS, 51). Not aware of Sue's discovery, Ramona flings a final mad arrogance at her as Sue flees: " 'Do you know what he said the last night when my name was Martha? The night he came into that room where the anemones were? He pretended that he was looking for a sheet of music. Specifically for a sonata for the harpsichord by Wilhelm Friedrich Bach' " (CS, 52). The implication of Ramona's speech is that Martha "died" because of an incestuous act, possibly with her father, whose memory caused her previously to flush and grow silent, or with one of her libertine brothers who had adored "Martha." Ramona's living death results from the degradation of her wealthy, Europeanized American family—the kind of evil explored by Henry James and no less forcefully portrayed by Stafford in her chilling revelation of Ramona's illness.

In "Maggie Meriwether's Rich Experience" (1955), Stafford displays another "innocent abroad." Maggie has more in common with Judy Grayson that she does with the other young women in Stafford's stories. "A simple country-club girl from Tennessee" (*CS,* 6), a member of Nashville's "young set," and a recent graduate of Briar Cliff, Maggie is on a year's tour of France. Her "rich experience" is an encounter with the superficial nastiness of a collection of Europeans gathered for a party at the fabulous Palladian demesne of Karl von Bubnoff, M. le Baron. Maggie is suffering a psychological aphasia, which has left her mute in French, and the other guests refuse to speak to her in English. In fact, they ignore her completely. Only twice does Maggie attempt to retaliate. After listening to the women discuss their favorite narcotics,[8] she recoils: " 'Have you-all ever tried snuff? You can lip it or dip it or sniff it. It's mighty good with sour mash or chips' " (*CS,* 11). Still ignored, she attaches herself to a nondescript man and delivers a bragging commentary on Vanderbilt University and the folk music of the Cumberland Plateau.

Maggie's American innocence and simplicity prove to be an undentable armor—as well as a substantial blinder—against which beat the decadence of M. le Baron's "marriage" to his estate, the casual discussion of drugs by the sophisticated women, the psychotic prince, the "French" lunch where "though the din was monolingual, it was that of Babel . . ." (*CS,* 12). Flustered, but unscathed and equally unenlightened, Maggie regales some young American friends with her day among the decadent and receives in reply their boisterously mistaken toast—to "the most sophisticated, the most cosmopolitan, the prettiest raconteur of Middle Tennessee" (*CS,* 17).

Stafford's first published story, "And Lots of Solid Color" (1939), is a fictionalized account of her attempts to find a teaching job after her return from Heidelberg. The story is particularly important in revealing her attitude toward her father, which she does not directly address again in her published work until "Woden's Day," which appeared posthumously. "And Lots of Solid Color" is clearly autobiographical. It is set in Portland, Oregon, where Stafford's parents had moved before she went to Heidelberg. Marie, the central character, has, like Stafford, two older sisters, one of whom lives on a ranch, as Stafford's sister did, and a brother, Johnny. Marie has just returned from spending a year at the University of Berlin. While she waits for replies to her application letters for teaching positions, she considers taking a job as a photographer's model.

Marie's father, like Stafford's, is a writer, and he is hopelessly out of touch with the realities of the publishing world as well as the rest of life:

All day she heard her father at his typewriter in the basement. *I think I'll write a review of Das Kapital for the Saturday Review of Literature.* But, Dad, they don't take things like that. *How about the New Yorker?* What can I say, Mother, when he makes such statements? *We'll be riding in a Packard pretty soon now.* For fifteen years (or was it fifty?) they had been hearing that. *The trouble with these damned editors is that they are afraid of new ideas, that's it. They won't take the penalty imposed on them by accepting real thought. Hell, yes, it's hard to get. Vague. Hell.* His flesh was melting away as he sat hour after hour at his typewriter quarrelling with Marx and Roosevelt, Christ and hundreds of others grouped into the general category of "abstractionists." His eyes were red from strain behind glasses that were wrong and could not be replaced.[9]

The pathetic portrait of the father, ineffectually dreaming, too poor to replace his glasses, exasperating in his unrealistic expectations, justifies the exhaustion and disillusion that Marie expresses when she thinks, "All my life, all my life, all my life I've heard those same words, *well, pretty soon we'll be riding in a Packard.*"[10] The hated ineffectualness of Kitty Winstanley's father, the absent or dead fathers of many other characters—all suggest the ambivalence Stafford felt about the father figure. The portrait of the father of the autobiographical Marie shows the roots of this ambivalence, just as Kitty Winstanley's bitterness at her mother's willful remaking of the world reveals Stafford's difficulty with the mother who has been forced to take control of the family.

The need for and the hopelessness of reconciliation with the estranged father is the theme of "A Reunion" (1944), published five years after "And Lots of Solid Color" and the third story Stafford published. The nameless heroine and narrator has come to visit her father in a nameless town. She was orphaned when her mother died at her birth. Her father has shaped his life, as well as the garden to which her mother's grave has been transferred, as a testimony to his great love and grief for his dead wife. The obverse of this love is hatred for his daughter, who is "the image of her mother."[11] The action takes place under a full moon in the consecrated garden, where seven years earlier the two had parted in bitterness. A beetle that her father half kills, amid their desultory conversation, which reveals that the reunion is not a reconciliation, symbolizes the narrator's own inarticulate struggles to "right" herself and stand her ground with her father. Later, the dead beetle lies like a human fetus, reminding her of the fate her father would have preferred for her had his wife been thereby saved.

The implied guilt felt by the narrator of "A Reunion" is the dominant emotion in "And Lots of Solid Color." Marie does not dwell, other than in the passages quoted, on her feelings about her father, revelatory as they are. She does brood on the special privileges, the education, she feels she has had at the expense of her family, particularly her brother Johnny: "As I was riding in a gondola, my brother was going hungry."[12] She remembers the letter: *"Dear Marie, it is not that we are asking for the money you borrowed, but we feel that you ought to be financially independent. Can't you get a job, just any kind? You are such an impractical dreamer."*[13] And she finds "it is too much to think about the whole family at once. . . ."[14] Her guilt increases her anxiety about obtaining a position; "her old sins, her lies, her blasphemies flowed back upon her. . . ."[15] The story ends without a resolution— with her receiving another rejection letter—and with Marie's seeming acceptance of her fate as God's punishment of her.

The real Jean Stafford did find a teaching position at Stephens College. "Caveat Emptor" (1956) is based on her experiences there. In the story she expresses the same scorn, in almost the same words, for the fictional Alma Hettrick College for Girls that she does for Stephens in her essay "What Does Martha Mitchell Know?" The stated aim of Alma Hettrick was " 'to turn out the wives and mothers of tomorrow.' These nubile girls, all of them dumb and nearly all beautiful, knitted in class (that is how they would occupy themselves in their later lives when they attended lectures, said the dean when Malcolm complained of the clack of needles and the subordination of the concept of doubt to purling); they wrote term papers on the advisability of a long engagement and on the history of fingernail polish . . ." (*CS*, 75).

Against this background, Victoria Pinckney, twenty-two, from

Maine, and Malcolm Kirk, twenty-three, from the Rockies, fall
charmingly in love. At first, engaged to other people, they simply
become attached as friends in alliance against the Alma Hettrick phil-
istinism. Stafford placed their story in *The Collected Stories* as the last
of the group under the heading "The Innocents Abroad." These innocents are abroad, however, "in the middle of the Middle West."
They find sanctuary each Sunday in a small town, Georges Duval's
Mill, whose original French settlers had been little touched by the
twentieth century and barely by the nineteenth.

The relationship between the two young people is closely scruti-
nized by the Alma Hettrick crowd. The latter considers them in love
(when they are not), estranged (when they are in love), and finally
hopeless dry-as-dust intellectuals when Victoria and Malcolm profess
that they are engaged in an academic study of Georges Duval's Mill
after the Alma Hettricks discover they are spending the whole of each
weekend there at a hotel.

Stafford wittily satirizes academics in her description of the
Georges Duval's Mill Project, which is undertaken by various Alma
Hettrick faculty members when that crowd decides that Victoria and
Malcolm "had no right to stake a claim on such a gold mine" (*CS*,
88). After Miss Firebaugh of the Personality Clinic discovers that
most clothes in the town are from Sears, Roebuck; the Child Study
Group discovers rampant incest and cretinism; the American History
people discover that no one knows anything about the origins of the
town; the Political Scientists find no politics; the Appreciation of Art
people find no art; and the Community Health class finds head lice
and a doctor who practices phlebotomy, the Alma Hettrick crowd
leaves the town alone: "It wasn't a question of missing the boat—the
boat wasn't there" (*CS*, 89). When Malcolm and Victoria announce
that they plan to continue their own philological and philosophical
studies, a guise for continuing their weekend trips, Alma Hettrick
washes its hands of them and plans not to renew their contracts—
leaving Malcolm and Victoria exactly as they wish to be, alone.

"Caveat Emptor" stands out in Stafford's stories of young women
for its lighthearted satire and its happy, but far from saccharine, ending. These innocents are among American philistines, presided over
by a Babbitt-like President Harvey, who prefers that the young
women students call him "Butch." The people Victoria and Malcolm
encounter are not evil, simply foolish and misguided. They are aca-
demicians who scorn intellectuals—and are proud of it.

After failing—in her eyes—as a teacher, Stafford fled east. In "The Bleeding Heart" (1948) Stafford reveals through the character of the young Mexican woman Rose Fabrizio the extent of her own feelings of isolation as an outsider in New England even as she had achieved her desire to get there. Rose, at twenty-one, has come to New England from the West, because "as far back as she could remember, she had been driven to get away, far away, and never go home again . . ." (*CS*, 156). Despite the misery that she feels half the time because she *is* an outsider, she nonetheless takes great joy in the complete difference from her home that she finds in New England.

The following contrast of East and West is the most specific one that Stafford makes in her fiction. Some of the "western" details appear in the Adams stories. Some of the "eastern" ones in *Boston Adventure*.

[Rose] rejoiced in the abundance of imposing trees, in the pure style of the houses and the churches, in the venerable graveyards and in the unobtrusive shops. One was not conscious of any of the working parts of the town, not of the railroad or of the filling stations or of the water towers and the light-plants. Her own town, out West, had next to no trees and those were puny and half bald. The main street there was a row of dirty doorways which led into the dirtier interiors of pool halls, drugstores where even the soda-fountain bar had a flaccid look, and small restaurants and beer parlors and hotels whose windows were decorated sometimes with sweet-potato vines growing out of jam cans painted red, and sometimes with a prospector's pick-ax and some spurious gold ore, and sometimes with nothing more than the concupiscent but pessimistic legend that ladies were invited or that there were booths for them. The people here in this dignified New England town, shabby as they might be, wore hats and gloves at all hours and on all days and they appeared moral, self-controlled, well-bathed, and literate. The population of her own town was largely Mexican and was therefore, by turns, criminally quarrelsome or grossly stupefied so that when they were not beating one another up they stared into dusty space or lounged in various comatose attitudes against the stock properties of the main street: the telephone poles and fire hydrants and hitching posts. They were swarthy and they tended, on the whole, to be fat and to wear bright, juvenile colors. Repudiating all that, she greatly admired the pallor of the people here and their dun dress and their accent so that the merest soda-jerk sounded as if he had gone to Harvard. (*CS*, 148)

The "truth" of this description is not particularly important, although, unfortunately, Stafford's stereotyping of the "Mexicans" is almost vicious. What is important is that Stafford chooses to allow her character such a distorted misapprehension of the relative validity of the two places and the two peoples. Rose's hatred of her origins must include a hatred of herself. It certainly includes a hatred of her father, whom she considers "stupid and cynical" and about whom "she did not know one good thing" (*CS*, 156). She remembers him wearing "a black coat-sweater from J. C. Penney's and a spotty gray cap and Army store pants and miner's shoes studded with cleats," carrying with him "the putrefied smell of sugar beets" even after his rare baths (*CS*, 156). When she is especially despondent, she thinks, "If my father had not been a low person and if he had loved me, I would not have grown up in poverty and I would not have hated him so much that I had to go away from home to the first job that came along . . ." (*CS*, 157).

In an unfinished and undated autobiographical novel set in a fictionalized Boulder, which she called "In the Snowfall," Stafford creates Joyce Bartholomew and her father, Fulke Bartholomew, a writer. The following description demonstrates the autobiographical basis for the feelings that Stafford transposes to Rose Fabrizio: "Joyce hates him and she is resentfully embarrassed by his infantile assumption that the same relationship exists between them that did when she was a little girl. . . . The very sight of him (he chews tobacco constantly, he seldom shaves, he is always dirty and as shabby as a hobo) is intolerable to her and she avoids him as much as possible. . . ." In a later passage, Stafford writes that Joyce feels that her parents had committed a "double crime" against her: "they had borne her and then had not provided for her."[16]

A corresponding portrait appears in "Woden's Day" (1979). This story was excerpted from Stafford's last unfinished novel, "The Parliament of Women," by her editor Robert Giroux and was published posthumously. The story records the history of the Savage family in Missouri, before they move to Adams, Colorado. It is interesting primarily for its portrait of Dan Savage, the character based on Stafford's father. He is portrayed, prior to his marriage to Maud McKinnon, as a well-educated young dreamer who ultimately decides that "he would be Vergil rather than Aristotle and when he was not upon his rural rides, overseeing his flocks and grain, his apiary and his vineyards, he would write: not idylls, not epic poetry but fiction and meditative essays. In time he would take a wife because he wanted sons, sons to teach, thereby combining all his talents, agrarian, literary, academic."[17]

The dream continued, as Stafford reveals in "And Lots of Solid Color." But his idyll did not come to pass in reality. He did write and publish some of his work. He did marry, but he had three daughters and only one son. He lost most of the property that would have allowed his Vergilian existence. When the family "began to be poor," Dan Savage changed, and Stafford describes him in the same terms in which years before she had described Fulke Bartholomew:

Dan's bilious moods came oftener, his "spells" were terrifying: one time he went into Hubbard's Dry . . . and inveighed against his father-in-law with such blood-curdling invective, such heart-splitting blasphemy that Mr. Hubbard himself ushered him out of the store like a hobo. And he looked like a hobo: barefoot, his long underdrawers showing beneath his unlaced cavalry britches: his hair was as long as William Jennings Bryan's and he hadn't shaved in a week; tobacco juice oozed down his chin from the quid he held in his cheek.[18]

His marriage was also troubled. The children did not understand why their parents did not separate and stop their "endless insults." They decide, "One of these sunshiny days we'll run away from them,"[19] an action that Stafford in fact carried out. Uncomprehending as children, when Cora (Stafford's name for herself) and her brother grow up they understand "how weak a man their father was for all his tempests and his brutality; and, seeing that, saw to their incredulity how strong their mother was, that often weepy, often quaking goose."[20]

In a desire to erase her past and become someone new, a desire that Stafford apparently shared based on the evidence of the autobiographical works, Rose Fabrizio longs to be adopted by a New Englander. In her need and in her ignorance, she selects as her foster father a man whom she sees three days a week at the town library and about whom she fantasizes an aristocratic life. This fantasy dissolves into horror when several months later she discovers that he lives in squalor next door to her with his "obscene" elderly mother and equally obscene elderly parrot; that his aristocratic ascot up close reveals the dinginess of many months' wear and covers the "most unsightly wen"; that his urging her to call him "Daddy" is the grotesque expression of an "elderly roué." He is literally, and figuratively, a dirty old man, no better, and ultimately worse, than her own real father. Rose is twice orphaned, once by her hatred and rejection of her father, once by the ignorance of her illusions.

If "The Bleeding Heart" can be seen as reflecting some of Stafford's feelings about her status as an outsider from the West isolated in the

East, "The Interior Castle" (1946) certainly describes the most physically excruciating event of her introduction to New England, her injury in the car accident in 1938. In this story, Stafford describes her
own suffering through the character Pansy Vanneman. Pansy's isolation from the world exterior to herself is almost complete. She is frozen in position, the image that Stafford uses for Ella in "The
Darkening Moon" and Cora Savage in "The Philosophy Lesson." Her
position signifies her rejection of a world that has caused her such
pain. Her immobility is "so perfect and stubborn . . . that it was as
if the room and the landscape, mortified by the ice, were extensions
of herself. Her resolute quiescence and her disinclination to talk, the
one seeming somehow to proceed from the other, resembled, so the
nurses said, a final coma" (CS, 181).

Pansy's face has been so badly cut up that the surgical stitching
makes it appear "darned," her nose has been smashed so badly it requires a complete reconstruction, and she has two major fractures of
the skull. Her injuries, however, do not require her immobility. She
herself wills it. It allows her to concentrate her thoughts on the only
remaining beauty left in her head, her brain—"not only the brain as
the seat of consciousness, but the physical organ itself. . . . It was
always pink and always fragile, always deeply interior and invaluable.
She believed that she had reached the innermost chamber of knowledge and that perhaps her knowledge was the same as the saint's
achievement of pure love" (CS, 182). Consoled by the comparison to
St. Teresa, Pansy is not, however, free from an assault on her own
"interior castle." It is caused by the preparation for the surgery on
her nose. Although she has prided herself on her deliberate excursions
into pain and her pleasure on returning from the exploration of it,
the pain associated with the surgery is beyond her control. It is "the
hottest fire, the coldest chill, the highest peak, the fastest force, the
furthest reach, the newest time" (CS, 192). Although Pansy breaks
her immobility in a futile attempt to ward off the violation of her
inmost secret, the assault is successful, the pain conquers, and Pansy
is left "within her treasureless head" (CS, 193).

In Pansy Vanneman, Stafford displays the young woman dehuman-
ized. Pansy suffers, as Stafford did, the almost literal loss of her face.
She is unrecognizable as the person she was. Consequently, she rejects
her outward form to focus on a fragile internal beauty, which she perceives in nonhuman images of jewels and flowers. When she plays
with the pain, she perceives her whole being as abstract or inanimate:

"Now she was an abstract word, now she was a theorem of geometry, now she was a kite flying, a top spinning, a prism flashing, a kaleidoscope turning" (*CS,* 189). Pansy is no longer human. She is a thing, however exquisite, at the mercy of others. The cost of regaining her humanity is the loss of the interior beauty she has created.

The stories about young women that are set in New York continue to reflect Stafford's own experiences, the time of her "Catholic work" and her long period of depression following her divorce from Lowell. In them, the young women, alone and outsiders, are assailed by people and circumstances that are emotionally and psychologically damaging. The unnamed heroine of "Between the Porch and the Altar" (1945), new to the city, steps apprehensively into the streets of the Lower East Side on her way to the first mass on Ash Wednesday: "While her feet were steady enough, her breath was erratic and her ears were fanciful, making her think she heard sinister noises behind the blank faces of the buildings. She looked straight ahead, fearful of what she might see in the dark doorways . . ." (*CS,* 407–8). She is prevented from carrying out her intentions—to contribute to the poor box and to light candles for the soul of her dead mother and for imprisoned friends in China—by the monstrous inhabitants of those fearful streets. By the doorway of a shop filled with grotesque objects, she is accosted by a derelict who effectively extorts from her most of the money she had intended for her pious purposes. Her rout is completed by an old crone, who drags her last dime from her in a "squalid commerce" before the altar of St. Francis Xavier. Along the way, she is bombarded by grotesqueries. She is distracted from her devotions by the sight of black stubble protruding from the coif of a nun. The church is "ugly and in bad taste. The statues were gaudy . . . and the crucifix was sentimental" (*CS,* 411). The "oppressively low" ceiling reminds her of a "dreary train shed" (*CS,* 413). A simple act of piety becomes a source of nightmare.[21]

When Emma, in "Children Are Bored on Sunday" (1948), ventures into the Metropolitan Museum one winter Sunday, she is ending a year of self-imposed solitude that is the result of a severe depression caused by her feeling of complete rejection by the "Olympian" intellectuals whose cocktail parties are jousting matches for the egos of artists, composers, and writers. Her insecurity as a newcomer to New York convinces her that in that crowd "she was thought to be an intellectual who, however, had not made the grade. . . . She knew, deeply and with horror, that she was thought merely stupid"

(*CS*, 378). She internalizes what she perceives as their assessment and considers herself a "rube." On this day, after a year of trying to walk and drink herself to exhaustion and sleep, she is terrified of meeting face to face a member of the intellectual crowd whom she sights in the museum: "In so many words, she wasn't fit to be seen. Although she was no longer mutilated, she was still unkempt; her pretensions needed to be cleaned; her evasions would have to be completely overhauled . . ." (*CS*, 377). Excellent satire though this is of intellectual snobbery, the effect of it on Emma has been real and intense. As she tries to continue her tour of the museum, before the canvases "swam the months of spreading, cancerous distrust, of anger that made her seasick, of grief that shook her like an influenza chill, of the physical afflictions by which the poor victimized spirit sought vainly to wreck the arrogant healthy flesh" (*CS*, 381).

The intensity of Emma's emotional pain corresponds to the intensity of Pansy Vanneman's physical pain. Her year of solitude is as severe a rejection of herself as is Pansy's escape into the world of inanimateness. She has perceived herself as besieged by the intellectuals of the city as surely as the young woman on the Lower East Side has been surrounded by human detritus. She is a victim of her isolation and her fears and has projected her hatred onto herself. She is, like most of Stafford's young women characters, acted upon rather than being capable of action herself.

The dominant portrait of the young woman that emerges in the stories is that of a passive victim. Within the context of the family, she feels estranged from or maimed by the loss of a parent or both parents. She responds most characteristically by ironic detachment or by guilt-ridden, sometimes suicidal, self-hatred. Outside the family context, she encounters a world that seems to have no place for her, where malignant or grotesque forces, either natural or human, prey upon her. The victories she wins are small ones and costly in emotional, psychological, or physical terms. The young women who differ from this dominant portrait and who escape relatively unscathed usually are those who are protected by the advantages of wealth and social position.

Boston Adventure

In her first published novel, *Boston Adventure* (1944), Stafford follows the life of Sonia Marburg from her childhood through young womanhood. Stafford gives Sonia an unbelievably melodramatic family situation out of which Sonia equally unbelievably rises. This heroine, unlike many other Stafford characters, triumphs, although her victory can also be seen as her enslavement. She triumphs by holding to a steely self-interest that overrides any considerations of family or friendship.

The prelude to *Boston Adventure* and to the character of Sonia Marburg is the novel Stafford finished in Concord when she first went East but never published.[22] An interviewer reports Stafford's appraisal of the novel in 1952: "The war came along and its slant wasn't topical enough. Thank Heaven, oh, thank Heaven, its author apostrophizes. It was not, in retrospect, a book she would like to have written."[23] The slant is, in fact, quite topical, but its subject matter would have been extremely distasteful to the American public in the early forties.

The central character of the untitled novel is Gretchen Marburg, twenty-one, a German-American student at the University of Heidelberg in the late thirties. Gretchen has always felt herself an outsider, a child who has been taunted by other children for her being German, a dude on the ranch to which her father has retired, a young girl disliked by her brother's friends. When she arrives in Germany, however, she finds a place for herself; she immediately embraces, and is embraced by, the young Nazis of Heidelberg. Through them, she is also able to work out her need for revenge for past slights to herself. She becomes an informer against people who do not support the Nazis, including her own brother Karl and several of his friends. Her love affair with a young German aviator is as much an attempt to prove herself loyal to the *Vaterland* as it is a true involvement of the heart. Motivated by hatred and vengefulness, Gretchen Marburg is not an attractive character. At the end, when her lover is killed fighting in Spain and she piteously asks God what she has done wrong, the reader does not feel the sympathy for her that the author apparently does. Instead, one is inclined to think that Gretchen gets exactly what she deserves. Perhaps Stafford intended to demonstrate the lengths to which a human being can be driven by rejection. The slights that Gretchen suffers, however, are completely out of proportion to the retaliatory action she takes.

Stafford incorporates Gretchen's rather chilling character traits, only slightly softened, into the character of Sonia. She also uses other details from the Gretchen Marburg novel in *Boston Adventure*. In the original novel, Gretchen's father is Herman Marburg from Würzburg, Germany. The Marburg family vacations each year at the Hotel Van-

couver in Seattle, where a Miss Pride also vacations. Gretchen's
mother exhibits signs of madness; she sleeps in her coffin, for example. Gretchen and her brother discuss a young Japanese woman, Kakosan Yoshida, who is loved by Heyjim Littlefield, an Indian friend
of theirs who is an orphan from near Tulsa.[24] In *Boston Adventure,*
Sonia's father is Hermann Marburg from Würzburg, Germany. Sonia
meets Miss Lucy Pride at the Hotel Barstow in Chichester where Miss
Pride vacations each year. Sonia's mother goes mad. Kakosan Yoshida
is loved by Sonia's childhood sweetheart Nathan Kadish. Gretchen's
embrace of the Nazis is transformed into Miss Pride's sympathy with
Hitler's persecution of the Jews.

Sonia Marburg, from the time she is ten years old, wants to shed
her family and poverty in Chichester, be adopted by Miss Pride, and
be given entrance to Boston aristocracy. She wishes for her parents'
deaths so that she might achieve her dream. She has to wait the eight
years of book 1 of the novel for the dream to come true. Her parents
do not die. Her father does desert the family when Sonia is twelve,
leaving her mother pregnant with a son whom she hates and torments
from the moment he is born until she has driven him to death. Her
mother sinks into the madness that has flashed from her even in earlier times when she was apparently sane, but driven to frenzy by her
husband's inability to give her the riches he had promised her and by
memories of her own wretched childhood in Russia. The child Ivan
dies, Sonia carries out a fake burial at sea in order to satisfy her
mother's delusions, her mother completely loses touch with reality,
Sonia arranges for her to be confined in an institution, and Sonia is
free at last. Throughout the eight years of this remarkable history,
Sonia remains steadfast in her desire to go to Boston and live with
Miss Pride.

The cold objectivity with which Sonia narrates the horrors of the
Marburgs' family life makes her protestations of pain and sorrow at
the loss of her father, the death of her brother, and the insanity of
her mother sound hollow, especially when she says she "took a cruel
and perverse pleasure" in "the remorse of her [mother's] inner soul"
when Ivan dies.[25] She also takes pleasure, she "laughed outright," in
doping her mother into insensibility. The hollow sound of Sonia's
emotional response persists because Sonia knows and the reader knows
that the gradual disappearance of her relatives brings her closer to
being adopted by Miss Pride.

Sonia views Miss Pride with the same objectivity. After Ivan's
death, Miss Pride does not respond to Sonia's plea for money to bury

the child. She instead lies about receiving Sonia's letter. Sonia's response reveals the ice in her blood:

My first reaction was . . . almost of disgust as for a few seconds she stood before me, not as that grand Bostonian to whose slightest favor I had aspired, but as a selfish old woman who, as a sop to her conscience, had brought me a potted plant. It seemed to me that she had aged remarkably since the past summer. Probably no change had taken place in her at all. It is difficult, in a wrinkled face, to compute how many new wrinkles have appeared in a year's time, or to see, in white hair, all the stages of its purification. It was, rather, that I had changed and my altered feelings had turned a spotlight upon the arthritic stiffening of her fingers from which she had removed the white gloves, the dessication and the yellow hue of her creased skin, the protruberation of her veins, the liverish patches on her wrists, the aridity of her thin lips. But a censor in me checked me before I had disarrayed her features beyond repair. . . . (154)

Despite her recognition of Miss Pride's true nature—"an old, ugly woman inspired by a tenuous and urbane evil" (225)—Sonia will take no chances on destroying her possibility of reaching her goal.

Sonia's hypocrisy and persistence pay off, and Miss Pride invites her to live in her house in Boston as her secretary. In book 2, Sonia relates her life on Pinckney Street. Despite the outward appearances of her position there, Sonia remains in control of her destiny. After a few months on Pinckney Street, Sonia, who *has* been received in Boston society but in her special role as Miss Pride's companion, realizes that she has gained an advantage in her relationship with Miss Pride that she will exploit when she needs to. When Miss Pride reveals an uncertainty about Sonia's loyalty to her, Sonia feels "a sense of power over her that allowed me to make a private reservation. I would stay with her *so long* as she upheld her part of the bargain and did not deprive me of my freedom in those hours which were not dedicated to her. For it had occurred to me that as she grew older she might become more demanding of my time" (312). Sonia is no more willing to put up with a tiresome Miss Pride than she has been to endure her own mother.

Sonia's life in Boston is dominated by her hatred of Miss Pride's niece, Hopestill Mather, whom she has detested since she saw her as a child at the Hotel Barstow, and a corresponding love for Philip McAllister, Hopestill's intended fiancé. Since she is conscious of her love for Philip only when Hopestill is around, it appears that it is

primarily motivated by a desire to attract Philip away from the hated
Hopestill. Her attraction to him has another perverse basis. She realizes in Boston that the deep love she has asserted that she has felt
for Nathan Kadish, a childhood neighbor in Chichester, was really
only a fascination she felt for a disfiguring birthmark on his face. And
she wonders if she "would have coveted Philip McAllister if he had
not been deformed" by a stiff back (340). She concedes that her attraction is a "symptom of an abnormal and somewhat repulsive nature
in myself" (340).

Following the announcement of Hopestill and Philip's engagement, Sonia begins to believe that she is no match after all for the
hidebound Bostonians and she begins periodically to sink into a vision of a red room in a manner that raises questions about her own
sanity. The room is the only place where she can feel herself in
control:

> The room had been a little random daydream which I could have again,
> or it was like a lengthened *déjà vue,* that evasive quasi-memory which is a
> sort of unlearned knowledge of the soul. I could, I knew, in time, name in
> its real place each object in the room, and I felt confident that even after my
> vivisection, the room would accomplish again its impeccable synthesis, a
> fused and incomprehensible entity. It was a sanctuary and its tenant was my
> spirit, changing my hot blood to cool ichor and my pain to ease. Under my
> own merciful auspices, I had made for myself a tamed-down sitting-room in
> a dead, a voiceless, city where no one could trespass, for I was the founder,
> the governor, the only citizen. (414)

Ultimately, Sonia triumphs. Hopestill dies following a fall from
horseback that she has deliberately caused. Philip hates Hopestill for
tricking him into a marriage to hide her illegitimate pregnancy. Miss
Pride promises to pay for the support of Sonia's mother, in exchange
for Sonia's promise never to leave her. And Sonia's mother becomes
catatonic, relieving Sonia of any further personal contact with her.
Sonia is left tied to Miss Pride, but that is a servitude she has sought.

Early reviewers and later critics have called *Boston Adventure* Proustian and Jamesian. And there are certain superficial resemblances in
style and subject matter to the works of these two. But this exposé
of the conflict of cultures and classes exemplified in the poor young
"foreigner" from Chichester and the Boston Brahmins, this satire of
the "small, dour world" of Beacon Hill, this journey through the

memory of a knowing child, is obscured by the critical labeling. In *Boston Adventure,* Jean Stafford was primarily getting her own revenge against the proper Bostonians who had rejected her even though she had married into a family that brought her a listing in the Social Register.

It is not difficult to perceive in Sonia Marburg, the outsider, Jean Stafford, the outsider. Sonia acquires her desire to live with Miss Pride when as a ten-year-old she works as a maid at the Hotel Bristow; Stafford had been a twelve-year-old maid at a hotel. Sonia writes a Stafford-like western story about a "steely blue-eyed foreman of the Lazy S$_4$" (79), which is rejected by her teacher. Her father reads *Riders of the Purple Sage* in German translation, wants to go west, and has made himself cowboy boots in preparation. Sonia reports that when Miss Pride spoke of the West, "it was not quite a void, but it was something stretching interminably behind one's back. . . . [S]he had been 'out' once, and had not the least desire to go again." She tells a friend: "I dare say their rugged life and bad climate make the people hardy. But I must confess I find the Rocky Mountains quite hideous, quite lacking in style. . . . Even if the landscape didn't offend me, though, I couldn't endure the place more than ten days at a time. There is a crackly feel in western speech that sets my teeth on edge" (460). The inclusion of these incidents and details and Miss Pride's comment have little really to do with the story of the Russian-German heroine. They do, however, reveal the slights the author had felt because of her own origins.

Stafford specifically satirizes the Lowells, indirectly by a reference to "the shabbiest delicatessen on Revere Street" (256), the not quite socially correct street on which Robert Lowell's parents had their home. Directly, she has Miss Pride comment, "The less said about Amy Lowell, the better" (167). She also has Miss Pride express dismay with a young poet who is a thinly disguised Robert Lowell:

Some young person, child of an old friend, had one day come to tea and had brought with him the Holy Sonnets of John Donne, and in spite of her protests, had managed to read one aloud to her. . . . a particularly passionate one. . . . The same young man had, she understood, taken to writing poems himself . . . and had composed some vicious lines on the Granary Burying Ground. The young man's "case" was a mystery to her because he had . . . come from a perfectly dignified family . . . [and] was directly descended from at least two of the illustrious skeletons in the yard. (168)

Stafford planned to write a sequal to *Boston Adventure* and did compose fragments of one under two titles, "Parliament of Women" and "The Dream of the Red Room." An additional indication that Stafford put much of herself into Sonia Marburg is revealed in an outline she composed for the sequel—obviously after her divorce from Lowell. The outline traces the marriage of Sonia and Philip in terms of the incidents of Stafford's own marriage to Lowell.[26]

Chapter Four
Maturity and Old Age

The fiction that portrays maturing women, women married, widowed, divorced, or alone by choice, women in their last years, develops characters who are generally more active in controlling the circumstances of their lives than are the girls and younger women that Stafford creates. Nevertheless, some of the characters are portrayed as victims, some as a result of their own detachment from or arrogance toward the world. Images of illness become prominent in this work. The real orphans in Stafford's other fiction give way mainly to the imagery of the orphan used to describe the lonely conditions of the older women. The apparent impossibility of a sustained and loving marriage relationship becomes an important theme. As with those about girls and young women, several of the stories reflect very closely Stafford's own personal history, her marriage to Robert Lowell, her divorces, her multiple illnesses. They also reveal her continuing sense of rejection by the Bostonian elite, which she turns into savage satire. Additionally, they reveal Stafford's own continuing sense of dislocation. All of the work is set east of the Rocky Mountains, in the places where Stafford lived out her own later life.

The Stories

A story published when Stafford was forty-nine reveals the need of even the mature woman who has established her own life to try to overcome her sense of isolation from her beginnings and to reestablish connections no matter how tenuous they may be. "The Lippia Lawn" (1964) is set in the mountains of the Cumberland plateau. The narrator, a nameless woman, spends an afternoon searching in the woods with an old neighbor, Mr. Oliphant, for trailing arbutus to transplant to his garden in the village. The old man's memories of how the woods once were before the mountain people began to raid them for plants to send to New York awaken memories for the narrator as well. Stafford supplies no age, no reason for the narrator's residence for the winter in the mountains, no indication of family relationship,

but the narrator's attempts to trace her memories of the arbutus iden-
tify her as an autobiographical character. She remembers the arbutus
painted on the china coffee pot of a landlady when she was a student
in Heidelberg. She is reminded of her childhood in Covina, California, and the strong resemblance to the arbutus of the lippia in her
family's lawn. Other ephemeral memories from her childhood follow,
along with facts she has been told but does not remember, such as
the eighty-acre walnut grove that stretched behind the California
house.

The narrator's lack of clear memories is contrasted to the old man's
vivid recollections of the mountains when he was a boy—"this place
was Eden!" (*CS,* 178). His consolation, "Anyhow, a man can call the
old things to mind," does not calm her own "disquieted" mind to
which his words are "like a phrase of music once admired and now
detested" (*CS,* 178). Mr. Oliphant's rootedness contrasts with the
narrator's wanderings, her memories gathered not only in California,
but Santa Fe, Denver, Chicago, Toledo, and New Orleans. When she
chooses, after all, not to dig up and bring back the arbutus from the
special place Mr. Oliphant sends her, she responds to her perception
of the plant's determination to remain rooted where it has always
been: "It was as though the root was instinct with will. There was
something . . . monstrous in its determination to remain where it
grew . . ." (*CS,* 177). The plant and Mr. Oliphant measure the narrator's own rootlessness—or the roots she has perhaps wished to escape by her wandering.

When Stafford bought the house in Damariscotta Mills in 1945
with her royalties from the sales of *Boston Adventure,* she believed for
a while that she had indeed stopped wandering and would have a
place of her own. Although that dream was quickly dashed, the
months she spent in Damariscotta Mills were particularly fruitful to
her as a writer. Three of her stories very closely record her own experiences while living there. The Kavanagh mansion, which adjoined
Stafford's property, provided the setting for *The Catherine Wheel.* She
used the name Kavanagh several times as a place name.[1] She also
wrote a descriptive essay, "New England Winter," published with
lavish illustrations in *Holiday* (February 1954), about winter in Maine
as she and Lowell experienced it. One of the stories she sets there is
a satire on the local inhabitants. The other stories reveal the deterio-
ration of her marriage.

"Polite Conversation" (1949) is a thinly fictionalized account of
Stafford's relationships with one set of her neighbors in Damariscotta

Mills. She and Lowell (who appear as Margaret and Tommy Heath in the story) lived across a narrow road from an Episcopalian bishop's widow and her "rambunctious" brood of grown and half-grown children. When she could no longer find excuses, Stafford would give in to the widow's invitations to tea, where they were often joined by an Episcopalian nun. "Polite Conversation" immortalizes the widow as Mrs. Wainright-Lowe and the nun as Sister Evelyn. Stafford is particularly cruel in describing Eva, one of the Wainright-Lowe children, home on summer vacation from her teaching job in Salt Lake City, who "gurgled like a stomach" after being applauded for her well-known love of children (*CS,* 129). The story satirizes the small-mindedness of Sister Evelyn and Mrs. Wainright-Lowe, the intensity of their concentration on their own village matters, the inanity of their conversation, and their inability to understand the Heaths' unwillingness (because they are writers and because they are trying to work) to join in all the projects thought up by the Wainwright-Lowes. Tommy Heath is impervious to them: "he had irrefutably replied [to Margaret] that he would not go today or any other day, because he was an eccentric" (*CS,* 123). But Margaret experiences the frustration of being sufficiently manipulated by the ladies to make her feel guilty for not complying with their wishes. She is helpless against them because of their inability to recognize the validity of any kind of life other than their own.

The other stories set in Damariscotta Mills describe, one indirectly, the other quite directly, the disintegration of Stafford and Lowell's marriage. "A Country Love Story" (1950) describes the hollowness and anger of the fifth year of the marriage of May, who is thirty, and Daniel, her senior by twenty years, a history professor who has just spent a year in a tuberculosis sanatorium. The two move from Boston to Maine at the insistence of Daniel's physician, despite May's own judgment that another year of isolation would be harmful to Daniel. May's judgment proves correct. What she did not recognize, however, is that the year would allow Daniel to drive her to the brink of questioning her own sanity.

In October, after a few months of pleasant, companionable work on their house and grounds, Daniel retreats to his study and closes May out of his life. The few conversations they have deteriorate into quarrels. Daniel refuses to recognize May's pleas to him for release from the isolation he has imposed upon her. He instead begins to accuse her of having "done something" that she is ashamed of while he was in the sanatorium and begins to suggest that she is going mad, a suggestion that remains with May as a "deep, bleeding injury" (*CS*, 140).

The effect of Daniel's treatment is to push May into "a weighty but unviolent dislike" of Daniel. More dangerous to her, she is pushed to the edge of madness, into fantasizing a lover whom she eventually "not only believed in . . . but loved . . . and depended wholly on his companionship" (*CS*, 141). She develops the guilt about this fantasy lover that Daniel tries to force on her about her supposed indiscretion. In a savage kind of irony, Daniel feeds her sense of disequilibrium by forgiving her "because you don't know how you persecute me" (*CS*, 142). He continues, by the time she has reached such a state of depression that she is insomniac, by telling her that "perhaps when this is over, you will know the reason why you torture me with these obsessions and will stop" (*CS*, 143).

On one of her nightly insomniac vigils, she hallucinates and clearly sees her fantasized lover sitting in the sleigh whose continued dilapidated presence on their front lawn has become a symbol of May and Daniel's inability to communicate and has also excited May's imagining of her lover. After this vision, she sleeps as if in a coma, dreams of her lover, and is awakened by Daniel's saying to her, "The winter is over, May. You must forgive the hallucinations of a sick man"; he begs her, "If I am ever sick again, don't leave me, May" (*CS*, 144). Her affair ends. The pale, fair head of Daniel bending over her as she awakes is the fair head of her lover, who had "seemed rather frail, for there was a delicate pallor on his high intelligent forehead and there was an invalid's languor in his whole attitude" (*CS*, 144). The return of the real Daniel is too late for May. She remembers his previous condescending treatment of her even before the long winter began. She knows the lover/Daniel she has fantasized will never appear. The terrible image Stafford uses to describe May's contemplation of her future life—"like an orphan in solitary confinement" (*CS*, 145)—reveals the utter hopelessness of her situation.

This story provided another opportunity for Robert Lowell to vent his own emotions about Stafford and their marriage. According to C. David Heymann, "The fiction provided fragments of the imagery for Lowell's 'The Old Flame' [1964], with its hint of the poet's second wife, Elizabeth Hardwick. A double link occurs in the poem in the lines, 'No one saw your ghostly / imaginary lover / stare through the window, / and tighten / the scarf at his throat.' Jean Stafford's imaginary lover had been mysteriously preempted by Elizabeth Hardwick . . . ," whose first novel was *The Ghostly Lover*.[2]

"An Influx of Poets" (1978), the last story published before Stafford's death, describes very openly the unhappy expanse of her marriage to Lowell and its ending weeks at Damariscotta Mills. It is so painfully autobiographical that it is difficult to view it separately as a work of art. Theron Maybank *is* Robert Lowell, Cora Maybank *is* Jean Stafford, Minnie Rosoff *is* Gertrude Buchman. Buchman did fly into Damariscotta Mills in a Piper Cub. In the summer of 1946, Stafford and Lowell did entertain various visiting poets, "baby bards . . . [who] would very soon usurp their elders' thrones and their dominions."[3] She did type and retype Lowell's poems as he changed an *a* to a *the*. Eileen Simpson was astonished that, in the midst of her own work, Stafford seemed to accept this responsibility for playing typist for Lowell without question.[4]

In the character of Cora, Stafford writes:

This was not the way I had planned the summer. We had limped painfully through the fifth year of our marriage, having changed the scene of our travail each year from the beginning. Cambridge was no better than New York, New York no better than Connecticut, Connecticut no better than Louisiana or the mountains of Tennessee. But we often limped on different routes, shedding our blood on sand and rocks miles apart. When we did meet in some kind oasis or quiet glade, we were at first shy and infatuated and glad, but the reunion did not last, the shade and water were part of a mirage, lightning smote and burned the hemlocks of our forest sanctuary.[5]

She had expected their lives to be different in the house in Maine she had bought and furnished for them as their own: "My parlor! My own! I bought the house, I bought the furniture, the student lamps, the cachepots, the milk-glass bowls I used for water lilies from the lake . . ." (43). She had seen it as a sanctuary from Theron's aberrant impulses resulting from his conversion to Catholicism: "immersed in the rhythms of Gerard Manley Hopkins the poet, [he] was explosively ignited by Gerard Manley Hopkins the Jesuit . . ." (49). Herself a convert at eighteen, Cora had not found in Catholicism what she was seeking. Despite her attempts to explain that she does not simply doubt, but repudiates the teachings of the Church, Theron insists on remarriage in the Catholic church and on Cora's performing the duties of the church: "He'd run hellbent for election into that blind alley . . . and yanked me along with him, and there we snarled like hungry, scurvy cats" (49).

"Supinely," the word Cora uses to describe her acquiescence to her husband's religious fervor, is also apt as a description of her reaction to what she at first perceives as merely a flirtation between Theron and Minnie Rosoff. Even before the summer had begun, there had been warnings that Cora's hopes for the new life in Maine were doomed. The delay caused by the remodeling and preparation of the house cooled Theron's enthusiasm for the planned move. Thus, by Christmas of the preceding year Cora "was a witch again, and all day and all night my God-fearing yokemate burned me at the stake in Salem. He was right. I made no plea for myself, for I had the tongue of an adder and my heart was black with rage and hate"(52). By the time Minnie arrives in Maine, Cora has spent the summer wracked by "brutish headaches," "lurching nausea," and insomnia, which she copes with by drinking herself to sleep. The day of Minnie's arrival, Cora has been to Boston for an examination to determine the cause of her headaches. The "appalling" diagnosis has been that they are caused by her mental state, which she perceives is caused by the conflict in her marriage.

Cora seeks a release from her pain by fantasizing an affair between Theron and Minnie: "Dishonored, I would ascend refreshed, putting aside the ruin of this marriage shattered so ignominiously by *the other woman,* by that most unseemly of disgraces, above all by something *not my fault,* giving me the uncontested right to hate him" (55). Never believing her fantasy will come true, she encourages what is already a reality. Cora's "sensible and wifely side" was pleased that Theron was enjoying himself and was perhaps losing some of his inflexibility. Her "hermit side," the "secret boozehead side, looked on the alliance with even greater pleasure: I was blissfully addicted to the fantasies the genie of the bottle contrived for me each night . . ." (56–58). She is shocked from her passivity when Theron dismisses her by saying, "I don't want a wife . . . I want a playmate" (60). Cora's fantasy has come true. She is "dishonored"; she does "taste the vilest degradation, the bitterest jealousy, the most scalding and vindictive rancor" (56). Most shattering must be her knowledge that she had cooperated in her own victimization.

The futility of finding a release in marriage from isolation and pain provides the theme for other stories. In "The Connoisseurs" (1952), Mary Rand, a wealthy orphan from Boise, Idaho, and her husband, Donald, who have sought in travel a substitute for a married life of real communion and commitment, reach the end of their travels and the end of their marriage. Both committed travelers, Mary and her husband had several times encountered each other by chance in Europe and in Asia while each was traveling alone. They had married at the close of a few weeks of traveling together and had continued their honeymoon travel until World War II intervened. Mary, however, had considered her traveling self "as a pilgrim with a goal. She felt certain that when, with her guide, she entered Eden, she would be content to let her passport molder and her trunk keys rust."[6]

When their enforced residence in the United States during the war reveals to Mary and Donald what their traveling has hidden—that they are in "obstinate and fundamental disaccord" on almost every subject conceivable (234)—they choose to continue to believe that once they can again begin traveling they will rediscover a previous joy. As they begin a trip across Loch Lomond, during a rancorous tour of Europe after the war, "each had imagined . . . they could calmly talk again and could, with dignity concede. The solution to everything might lie on the farther bank; there was the possibility that in a tea shop in Inversnaid they might, in sudden revelation, learn how to accept" (198).

The deus ex machina that finally saves them from their endless, loveless wandering is another traveler, a bore and a boor, who attaches himself to them on the morning of their Loch Lomond excursion. His endless monologues about his own travels, his boring anecdotes, his praise of Iceland above all places, because it is absolutely ugly and filled with nothing, not only prevent any of the wished-for communication between Donald and Mary but also grotesquely parody the Rands' own travels, their inability to find a paradise to which they can commit themselves. The Englishman's intrusions into their illusions brings them up short against a reality they had refused to admit, "that they had long since ceased to love each other and their guilt over their failure, constant and inadmissible, had wedded them far more rigidly than any marriage vows" (240). The experience with the grotesque Englishman strips away their final pretense: "Politely on the bus they discussed Reno although, for the sake of the Englishman's *idée fixe,* they called it Reykjavik" (246).

Beatrice Trueblood's experience of marriage drives her into an isolation that, ironically, frees her from what she finally perceives to be the most unbearable and the most characteristic reality of marriage. "Beatrice Trueblood's Story" (1955) begins starkly: "When Beatrice Trueblood was in her middle thirties and on the very eve of her second marriage, to a rich and reliable man—when, that is, she was in the prime of life and on the threshold of a rosier phase of it than she had ever known before—she overnight was stricken with total deafness" (*CS*, 385). The "story" that leads to her deafness is a history of being traumatized by marital discord. As a child, she had nightly endured quarrels between her father and her alcoholic mother, who heaped "atrocious abuse upon each other, using sarcasm, threats, lies—every imaginable expression of loathing and contempt. They swam in their own blood, but it was an ocean that seemed to foster and nourish them; their awful wounds were their necessities" (*CS*, 402). Not convinced that marriage must be like this, she entered her own first marriage determined not to be a party to such scenes. Unfortunately, Tom Trueblood fed on "rancor and contentiousness." After seven years of having "her dignity trampled to death, her honor multilated," her only escape was to run away, leaving behind a note (*CS*, 403).

Beatrice's engagement to the wealthy Marten ten Brink is celebrated in Newport.[7] Her host, Jack Onslager, is the only one of her friends and acquaintances who realizes the tension between Beatrice and her lover, because it is revealed only on her face; it "was so still it could have been a painting of a face that had been left behind when the woman who owned it had faded from view" (*CS*, 391). After the two have quarreled the night through, standing below Onslager's window, Onslager overhears the following exchange, which settles Beatrice's fate: to ten Brink's command, "You mustn't think you can shut your mind to these things. . . . You can't shut your ears to them," Beatrice replies, "I will not hear another word" (*CS*, 392).

She does not. She escapes from what seem the inescapable quarrels of people who should love each other—and particularly ten Brink's outrageous jealousy of her first marriage—by willing herself deaf. She deliberately isolates herself from a cacophony that has literally become unbearable. She escaped from the psychological bloodbath of her parents' marriage, only to enter a mutilating marriage of her own. She does not receive the paradoxical sustenance her parents and her husband find in abuse. She flees into deafness to prevent a return to yet another degradation. Ironically, however, she is not finally able to break the cycle. Over a year later, after her hearing returns, she marries again. Once again it is Jack Onslager who finds the truth of Beatrice's new life when he overhears her husband say: "I have told you a thousand times that my life has to be exactly as I want it. So stop these hints. Any dedicated scientist worth his salt is bad-tempered"

(*CS*, 405). Beatrice Trueblood has reentered the only kind of relationship she has ever known.

In 1948 and in 1953, Stafford went to the Virgin Islands to obtain divorces from her first and second husbands. In 1949 and in 1955, she published stories that reflect, if not her actual experiences, her emotional responses to these events. The sordidness and the humiliation that accompany divorce is the theme of "A Modest Proposal" (1949). The setting is one of the Virgin Islands, where women waiting to be divorced are perceived in terms of flotsam and illness; they "littered the terrace and the lounges of the hotels, idling through their six weeks' quarantine. . . . They were spoken of as invalids; they were said to be here for 'the cure' " (*CS*, 66). Sophie Otis, from Massachusetts, is one of the favored "invalids" to have been invited by a local sybaritic Danishman to share his hospitality at his country home. During the course of an afternoon, she sits apart and observes the rest of the group, her fitting companion on the terrace a ruined head of Pan lying face down on the ground, a mocking symbol of the love that had brought the women eventually to where they are.

Mrs. Otis feels anesthetized and doomed to an unending exile, caught in the oppression and lonely heat of the windless Caribbean day. Trapped as they all are, by loneliness, by hopelessness, by futility, the guests are subjected to a revolting parody of Swift's essay— an apocryphal tale of their host's best friend serving him a charred baby islander for dinner. The tale especially torments the most fragile of the women guests, whom the host has deliberately provoked throughout the afternoon with his references to "coons," "niggers," and "jigaboos," just as he has subjected his other guests to sexual innuendos. The Danish captain's prized civilization is a guise that allows him to trample the humanity not only of his guests but also of the islanders, including his houseboy. It contrasts starkly with the islands and the cays Mrs. Otis views from the terrace: "They were intractably dry, and yet there was a sense everywhere of lives gathering fleshily and quietly, of an incessant, somnolent feeding, of a brutish instinct cleverer than any human thought" (*CS*, 69). The only recognition of her own and others' humanity and dignity comes from the captain's abused houseboy: "His was all the sufferance and suffering of little children. In his ambiguous tribulation, he sympathized with her . . ." (*CS*, 74).

"The Warlock" (1955) also emphasizes the humiliation that women seeking divorce are subjected to. The seemingly inescapable maltreatment is magnified in this instance because the woman so treated is not in fact intending to get a divorce. Mrs. Mark Kimball is traveling to Antigua to visit friends and to recuperate from a long illness. Because she is traveling alone, at Christmas, on a ship that frequently transports divorcées-to-be to the Virgin Islands, she cannot convince anyone that she is not seeking a divorce. A natural reticence and a guilty conscience prevent her from discussing her illness. It may have been an "unconscious blackmail" to restore a marriage that was on the brink of dissolving. Because of it, she will never be sure "whether it had been pity for her in her weakness and fear or the restitution of his married love that had brought [her husband] back to her from a long and serious digression."[8]

The cruise that was to be the beginning of her restoration to health becomes a nightmare of dingy accommodations crowded with irritable and noisy passengers presided over by a scabrous crew whose captain takes more interest in a blonde passenger than in the safety of his ship. Mrs. Kimball's reticence, a bout of flu, and her fragile sense of her relationship to her husband subject her to the raucous innuendos of her cabinmate, who is happily on her way to a divorce, and, worse, to the unwanted and constant attention of the ship's doctor, the warlock of the title. The incredible Dr. Cortez lives in rococo splendor in the midst of the prevailing shabbiness of the ship. His interest in the arcane allies him strangely with the voodooism of the tropics rather than with the world of modern medicine that he supposedly represents. Mrs. Kimball cannot, however, offend or ignore the doctor: "she might need his care and she did not like to think of a hypodermic needle in the hands of an enemy. . . ."[9]

Her sense of self is so fragile that she is relieved from her anxiety only by a cable from her husband saying he will meet her in Antigua. Finally freed from her fear of pursuit by Dr. Cortez, she takes on herself some of the blame for his reprehensible behavior; she is "partly ashamed" as well as "partly puzzled." She may have completely imagined a sequence in which she has felt him following her and observing her when she left the boat for an excursion, a possibility that suggests the illness attending the dissolution of her marriage may have been mental. The matter remains ambiguous, however, for as she last glimpses Dr. Cortez, he says, "I follow the pipes of Pan."[10]

A widow is the character chosen by Stafford to display the ability of a mature woman to act decisively to dispel a sense of being a victim. Abby Reynolds, in "The Children's Game" (1958), is a New Yorker in her early forties. She has spent the year following her husband's death in Europe, moving from place to place. She finally realizes that she has become one of the "forlorn, brave orphans"— lonesome American women—that she and her husband had seen and sorrowed for on their earlier trips abroad (*CS*, 22). She belongs to "that group who have spent their lives leaning on someone—or being leaned on by—a father, a mother, a husband; and who, when the casket is closed or the divorce decree is final, find that they are waifs" (*CS*, 22). They are humiliated in their loneliness and flee from the pity of their relatives and friends. In making her own trip, Abby has followed a pattern set by other women of her family, including her mother, who died in Rome.

Abby, however, finds that she is made of sterner fiber. She admits to herself that she hates what she is doing and resolves to return immediately to New York and her previous life. In the two weeks that intervene before her return passage, she agrees to meet an old friend, Hugh Nicholson, at a house party in England. Spending time with Hugh, Abby discovers that the enervation she has experienced was caused by "the removal from her life of John's energy" and that she requires the complement of such an energy; "she was not the sort of woman who could live alone satisfactorily" (*CS*, 25). She is a woman who needs a husband.

Stafford sets the final development of Abby's resolve against the grotesque casino town of Knokke-le-Zoute in Belgium. The casino and its occupants are described in the imagery of sickness. The international collection of roulette players appear "chronically ill"; they all resemble "the invalid concentrating on the tides of his pain" (*CS*, 19). The "air of apprehension and constraint" in the casino is appropriate to a hospital ward (*CS*, 19). The building is seedy and there is a "contagion in the atmosphere" (*CS*, 20–21). The town itself is "monstrous," with "houses that looked like buses threatening to run them down and houses that looked like faces with bulbous noses and brutish eyes" (*CS*, 29). Trees are cut into shapes of inanimate objects. The hotels take on a horrible animation with "kidney-shaped balconies, . . . crenellations that looked like vertabrae and machiolations that looked like teeth" (*CS*, 29).

Brought to Knokke-le-Zoute and the casino by Hugh, with whom she believes herself in love, Abby discovers that the grotesquerie about her reflects the sickness at the core of Hugh, a compulsive gambler, whose addiction has destroyed his first marriage. Hugh has brought her here to reveal this truth about himself. After playing an evening of roulette at Hugh's request, she understands the pull of the game to the gambler and with only a shade of remorse, "because she was fortunate and he was not" (CS, 33), she leaves him with hardly a backward glance. Her brief interlude has been an "aberration," like the quixotic change of the roulette wheel. She belongs among her own kind: "in alien corn, it was imprudent to run risks" (CS, 33).

In the stories of two other women in their forties, Stafford explores again the themes of isolation and disengagement. The emotional withdrawal for each woman has a different source but for each the result is a life of sterility. In "The End of a Career" (1956) Stafford satirizes the American emphasis on youth and beauty through the tragic story of Angelica Early. Praised and prized from her birth for her great physical beauty, Angelica is cut off from all other human understanding and enrichment, love, intellectual development, even close friendship. For Angelica, "aware of her responsibility to her beholders, dedicated herself to the cultivation of her gift and the maintenance of her role in life with the same chastity and discipline that guide a girl who has been called to the service of God" (CS, 448). Her puzzled friends cannot see that she has married the man she has precisely because he *is* away most of the time and does not interfere with the ritual required to maintain her beauty. She remains childless for doubtless the same reason. Her only real friend and confidant is her maid, her accomplice in maintaining her beauty.

Her acquaintances require nothing of her but that she be beautiful. Hostesses plan parties around her beauty. Men happily escort her for the reflected glow. That she offers little beyond her beauty matters not. That her vocation has robbed her of normalcy is unnoticed: "she had been obliged to pass up much of the miscellany of life that irritates but also brings about the evolution of personality; the unmolested oyster creates no pearl. Her heart might be shivered, she might be inwardly scorched with desire or mangled with jealousy and greed, she might be benumbed by loneliness and doubt, but she was so unswerving in her trusteeship of her perfection that she would not allow anxiety to pleat her immaculate brow or anger to discolor her damask cheeks or tears to deflower her eyes" (CS, 450–51). What Angelica perceives is that her friends expect her beauty never to change.

When at forty age inevitably begins to alter her, she fights more desperately to slow it, undergoing yearly and extremely painful facial restorations. Finally, her hands, which cannot be restored, show her years. With no resources open to her, with no sense of herself apart from her beauty, Angelica Early takes to her bed and dies, "her heart past mending" (*CS*, 463).

Forty-three-year-old Jenny Peck, in "I Love Someone" (1952), has remained a spinster by choice. She lives isolated from the passion of the world, symbolically in her apartment high above the Manhattan streets where young gangsters torture each other, and emotionally in a heart that does not allow itself to feel love. Contrary to the myths her friends have created about her single state, Jenny is honest about herself: "From childhood I have unfailingly taken all the detours around passion and dedication; or say it this way, I have been a pilgrim without faith, traveling in an anticipation of loss, certain that the grail will have been spirited away by the time I have reached my journey's end. If I did not see in myself this skepticism, this unconditional refusal, this—I admit it—contempt, I would find it degrading that no one has ever proposed marriage to me. I do not wish to refuse but I do not know how to accept. In my unforgivingness, I am more dead now, this evening, than Marigold . . ." (*CS*, 418).

Moved from her routine by the funeral of her friend Marigold, who has inexplicably committed suicide, Jenny is attracted to the sounds of a gang beating occurring in the area way below her window. She not only looks out and watches the fight to the end, but also attempts to pursue the gang once it leaves: "to see if I can penetrate at last the mysterious energy that animates everyone in the world except myself" (*CS*, 422). For once she is breaking from her "always rational behavior," which brings her no hope but also no despair. When she reaches the street, she is stopped by a childishly scrawled heart with a "fading proclamation, I LOVE SOMEONE." She sees in it a comment on her need for understanding of herself and other human beings: "As easily it could read, beneath a skull and crossbones, I HATE SOMEONE" (*CS*, 422). She feels no need to search further. She returns to the well-appointed banquet that is her life, which ironically lacks "something to eat" (*CS*, 422).

In three stories of elderly women, Stafford explores the results of both willful innocence and willful malevolence. In "The Captain's Gift" (1946) Stafford writes of the folly or perhaps the evil of a willful state of innocence which ignores evil. Mrs. Chester Ramsey, "an innocent child of seventy-five," resists change of all kinds. She refuses to move from her house on the Lower East Side of Manhattan, although it has been condemned by the fire department and is surrounded by slums. She dresses as her mother dressed a generation before, an eccentricity that sometimes she feels renders her "invisible" to the anonymous and motley crowd that throngs the once elegant square on which she lives. Above all, she refuses to recognize that World War II is being fought. She is unmoved by this cataclysmic fact despite her correspondence with several young men who are fighting in Europe and the reality that all her children and grandchildren are involved in some way in the war effort.

Mrs. Ramsey has lost all trace of any physical beauty, but she is known for her charm, which brings frequent visitors to her unsuitable house. The charm lies in "her tenderness and pity, her delicate and imaginative love, her purity that makes her always say the right thing. . . . She has neither enemies or critics, so that like an angel she is unendangered by brutality or by 'difficult situations' " (CS, 440). Mrs. Ramsey's "purity" and innocence, however, do at last provoke brutality, from her favorite grandson, Arthur, who has been fighting in Europe. While he has sent her many affectionate letters and says he knows he will find her unchanged when he returns, he finally writes from Germany that he is sending her "the best present" he has yet found for her. When it arrives, it proves to be a long golden braid, cut from the nape of a girl's neck. Shaken, Mrs. Ramsey says aloud, "How unfriendly, Arthur," but through the "present" his message comes to her, "There's a war on, hadn't you heard?" (CS, 445).

"The Hope Chest" (1947) portrays the painful loneliness of an irascible, impossible spinster, Miss Rhoda Bellamy. Despite her parents' wealth and social position, her debut into Boston society had been such a fiasco and such a "sensational" miscarriage that the family moved to Maine, her mother dying soon thereafter. There, on Christmas Eve of her eighty-second year, her need for human love brings Miss Bellamy to extort a kiss from a small boy in exchange for buying from him a homemade Christmas wreath. As she lies in bed on Christmas morning remembering where the wreath that disfigures her elegant wallpaper has come from, her thoughts reveal that her loneliness results from her own overbearing arrogance—possibly the cause

of her disastrous debut, certainly the cause of her unnatural attachment to her father, who through their long years together had been
her only "beau." At last, she remains true to her lifelong nature and
uses her cantankerousness to hide her deep hurt, which she lies nurs-
ing "like a baby at a milkless breast, with tearless eyes" (*CS,* 119).

Equally cantankerous, and sadistic, eighty-year-old Isobel Carpenter, in "Life Is No Abyss" (1952), spitefully lives in the poorhouse in
order to cause as much pain as possible to her Cousin Will for losing
her fortune in bad investments. Isobel is also a spinster; she pro-
claims, "I was too good to get married. . . . I was too good and too
rich" (*CS,* 190). Her insistence on staying in the poorhouse, despite
numerous and frequent offers by various wealthy cousins for her to
live in their homes, contrasts grotesquely—even evilly—with the
hopelessness of those who are there because they have no choice. In
the large ward which Lily Holmes, Isobel's twenty-year-old cousin,
can view from Isobel's bedside, "every bed—and there were four long
rows of them—was occupied by an ancient, twisted woman; the
humps of their withered bodies under the seersucker coverlets looked
truncated and deformed like amputated limbs or mounds of broken
bones, and the wintry faces that stared from the stingy pillows had
lost particularity; among them it would have been impossible to determine which was primarily bleak or mean or brave or imbecile, for
age and humiliation had blurred the predominant humor and had all
but erased the countenance" (*CS,* 101) Closer by, Isobel's roommate
Viola, a blind, perhaps mentally defective, woman presents to Lily a
"generic face . . . a parody, the scaffolding of ageless bone; it was an
illustration, a paradigm of total, lifelong want" (*CS,* 104).

Lily, an orphan, penniless herself, but a ward of Cousin Will, is
taunted by Isobel that she too will wind up in the poorhouse: "The
lack of money is everything. . . . The lack of money is the eternal
punishment" (*CS,* 110). Isobel's total disregard of the genuine pain
and suffering of the other inmates of the institution is revealed in her
taunt. Lily, who has felt herself "drowning" as Isobel has dispassion-
ately described the screams of dying old people, turns finally on Isobel and in doing so accurately describes the old woman: "You are a
vulture! You haven't got a drop of love in you!" (*CS,* 110). Privileged
herself, however, Lily's thoughts of the paradoxical situation she has
viewed between her hateful, spiteful old cousin and her roommate
Viola, whom Lily thinks is the "only person who has love . . . who

can't take anything and can't give anything" (*CS*, 112), are rapidly erased by the sight of her favorite beau waiting for her return. Life is, after all, no abyss—for the privileged few.

"A Winter's Tale"

This novella is narrated by Fanny, who at thirty-seven is married, apparently happily, to a lawyer in Cambridge and has a son and a daughter with whom she is apparently on good terms. The story she tells, however, is not the story of her marriage and family. It is the story of the winter of the year she spent in Heidelberg as a student. That time is recalled to her by her finding a jacket with a seashell in the pocket, both of which had been given to her by a young man she had loved in Heidelberg.[11] For several days, Fanny sits in the late afternoon, drinking whiskey and removing "the winding sheets from the dead days" (*BC*, 226).

The story Fanny tells is Stafford's final version of the unpublished Gretchen Marburg novel. In it Fanny replaces Gretchen as the young American woman who falls in love with one of Hitler's aviators. Fanny's love for Max Rössler is innocent and apolitical, unlike Gretchen's for Rheinhard Rossler. Fanny, an Irish Catholic Bostonian, has been sent to Heidelberg by her father to study German, while he spends his own sabbatical in Paris. Fanny's mother had died at her birth and she is "kithless except for Daddy and the spinster aunts and lonely all through childhood" (*BC*, 232). Consequently, she goes to Heidelberg intending to have a love affair: "I did not mean to love. I meant to be 'in love' and to be sorry when it was all over . . ." (*BC*, 253). She finds herself, however, loving Max Rössler.

The relationship between Fanny and Max is immensely complicated by Max's involvement with Persis Galt, the woman into whose care Fanny's father has placed her. In Persis Galt, Stafford develops the reprehensible qualities she has given Gretchen Marburg in the unpublished novel. She also uses Persis Galt as a symbol of the kind of evil that Beacon Hill can produce. Like Miss Rhoda Bellamy in "The Hope Chest," Persis was "born well, born rich, presented to society by trusting parents, had been a singular failure . . ." (*BC*, 231). She received no suitable marriage proposals. In retaliation, she had flirted with Catholicism, married an atheist, and finally converted after she arrived in Germany. Although her husband is a Scot, she has become so thoroughly "Teutonized" that she prefers to be addressed as Frau Professor Galt, and she dresses the role in "good, gloomy tweeds, a stout pair of driving gloves, lisle stockings with a lavender cast and common-sense oxfords with heavy soles" (*BC*, 233). She has become equally Catholicized, to the point of surrounding herself as often as possible with Benedictines from the nearby monastery and considering one her own "private" monk. When she dresses to entertain them, however, she wears a provocative long black velvet dress with a low neckline and tight bodice.

Despite her apparent rejection of both her country and the religion of her birth, Persis Galt retains the arrogance of her Bostonian upbringing. She tells Fanny, "There's far more *mingling* in Europe than in Boston," and Fanny recognizes that "by opposing a whole continent to a single city she proclaimed herself inalienably Bostonian, however Popish her metaphysics, however Bavarian her walking shoes . . ." (*BC*, 236). When Fanny first sees her, Persis, in her middle forties, looks to Fanny "exactly like the purposeful matrons in black Persian lamb marching down Beacon Street on their way to lunch at the Chilton Club" (*BC*, 233). She has also re-created a Beacon Hill interior for her German house.

Fanny learns from Mellie Anderson, another young woman who has been placed in the care of Persis, that Persis uses her position to spy on and control the young woman by reporting any slight deviation in Mellie's behavior to her mother. Similarly, she controls her own family with her money, even though Persis "loathed all her family and they all loathed her" (*BC*, 246). Finally, Fanny learns that Persis controls Max Rössler, who tells Fanny that "sooner or later everyone who crosses that threshold gets blackmailed unless they're too disabled, in one way or another, for her to bother with" (*BC*, 260). When Fanny meets Max, Persis has been his mistress for five years, the last four of which he has hated her. Max believes Persis has seduced him "to make up for a lack of talent . . . for being good. In the absence of goodness, she had to have power, and who could be better controlled than an eighteen-year-old weakling?" (*BC*, 259–60).

Within these terms, Fanny and Max conduct their own love affair. Fanny recalls, "There was no pleasure in it, I suffered perpetually, it was monstrous to live through, but I could not have escaped it, not possibly" (*BC*, 262). At Christmas in Freiburg, when Fanny last sees him, she finally learns the hold Persis has on Max. He is a Jew. The hopelessness that Max feels leads him to decide to die when he leaves Fanny in Freiburg to go to fight in Spain. Fanny perceives his determination to die as also a rejection of her. She acts out her own rejection by having "a wonderful time" on the day she receives the notice of his death. But she spends her last months in Heidelberg in a "heavy stupefaction." Seventeen years later, as she muses for the last time on that winter love, she finally lays her lingering guilt to rest: "I think, my God, Jew or not he was a Nazi; and then I think, what did Nazi mean when I was twenty?" (BC, 276).

In "A Winter's Tale" Stafford makes the substance of the Gretchen Marburg novel not only palatable but powerful. She creates in Persis Galt perhaps the most evil character in her fiction. She assigns to her the feelings of rejection and the need for revenge that are found in a number of her other characters. But she allows Persis, the hypocritical Bostonian, actually to carry out that revenge, to the point of causing her unwilling lover's death. By clothing Fanny's love for Max in a naive innocence, she creates a different response to Fanny's last question than she does to Gretchen Marburg's piteous plea. When Fanny tosses the seashell through her bedroom window, the ghosts of her past are expunged.

The Catherine Wheel

The Catherine Wheel (1952), whose heroine is thirty-eight-year-old Katherine Congreve, is Stafford's only published novel that focuses on a mature woman. Katherine is unchanging, like Mrs. Ramsey in "The Captain's Gift," wearing eccentric clothing of a generation before, riding in 1936 in a brougham, attended by a liveried footman. She is single, to the astonishment of all her friends and relations, her niece believing, as Cousin Isobel has said of herself in "Life Is No Abyss," that "no one in the whole wide world was good enough for her."[12] She has clothed herself in an ironic detachment, like Jenny Peck in "I Love Someone," an attitude learned from her father, "so endowed with control and tact and insight and second sight that the feelings that might in secret ravage the spirit could never take the battlements of the flesh; no undue passion would ever show . . ." (66). She resides from May to October at Congreve House, her summer home in Maine, eschewing the more fashionable resorts of her wealthy Boston friends and relatives. Each summer at Congreve House she entertains her young cousins Honor and Harriet and Andrew while their parents John and Maeve Shipley tour Europe.

Beneath the surface of Katherine Congreve's well-ordered and civilized life, however, burn those "undue passions" that the civilized person never shows. She is unchanging because for her time stopped on the night twenty years before when she realized that John Shipley, whom she deeply loved but to whom she had never revealed her feelings, had instead fallen in love with her cousin Maeve. In a parody of T. S. Eliot, a selection from whose *Murder in the Cathedral* is the epigraph for the novel, Katherine says, "There is only one time . . . and that is the past time. There is no fashion in *now* or in *tomorrow* because the goods has not been cut" (43). Her anecdotes follow no chronology. They move "as if from case to case in a historical museum" (43) or as if one were viewing a Chinese painting: "there was no progression in time because there was no perspective and therefore no shrouding of the past; the present was exactly the same size as the past and of exactly the same importance and except in the most minor and mechanical of ways, the future did not seem to exist" (44). The passionate love that froze time for Katherine has been so well hidden by her that the Shipleys took her along on their honeymoon and the three have remained a fashionable and inseparable "threesome" in Boston ever since.

Katherine's passions have also been fed by an ugly resentment of Maeve, not only for winning John's heart while unaware of Katherine's feelings, but for incidents from much earlier in their lives. Maeve entered the Congreve family as an orphan, a ward of Katherine's father. The two girls had been reared as sisters. During a time when Katherine's father had been having an affair, he showed especial fondness for Maeve, who "was not the daughter of the wife whom he did not love" (213). Later, when the girls were in school in France, Katherine's "greatest joy" was receiving letters from her father while Maeve wept at receiving none. Katherine thus got her revenge for the earlier slight. But the resentment of Maeve remained. Katherine "had never really forgiven Maeve for those two or three years when she had been [Congreve's] darling. The fact was that she had never really forgiven poor Maeve for anything. . . . In Katherine, a grown and apparently integrated woman, there bitterly rankled still the recollection of how all the young men in her girlhood had been taken first with her and every one of them had abandoned her the moment they met Maeve, who was not more beautiful, not more alert, danced no better" (214).

Thus, in the winter before this last summer Katherine is to spend at Congreve House, Katherine accepts John Shipley's declaration of

love and offer of marriage—if at the end of the summer he still does
not wish to remain with Maeve. Her acceptance is not joyful. Instead, she "somberly contracted to revenge for her ancient wound. . . .
[She] was and had always been 'in love' with John Shipley and she
knew that at the moment of conjugal commitment, the state of being
in love would be annulled and she would never be accessible to him
again through any ruse . . ." (93–94). In the course of the summer,
during which she sees John's return parodied by the proposals of another of her old lovers, she decides she need not marry John, because
she has already accomplished her purpose. She admits to herself:
"what I wanted I have now achieved, my desire is consummated for
I have supplanted Maeve . . ." (219).

Paralleling and entwined with Katherine's own innerly tumultuous
last summer at Congreve House is the equally savage emotional experience of her twelve-year-old cousin Andrew Shipley, who nurtures
a hatred of the older brother of his only summer friend. Andrew al-
ternatively makes incantations urging the brother's quick death and
prays for his quick recovery, either way to remove him from Hawthorne so that Andrew can have his friend Victor as a playmate again.
Small, shy, bookish, and dreamy, Andrew is without friends in the
winters in Boston. He resents his older sisters for past slights to him.
He hates his father. He cannot "imagine ever being in the least interested in any member of his own family, except Cousin Katherine
. . ." (29). Combined in Andrew, one sees the most awkward and
resentful and angry moments of Ralph and Molly Fawcett in their
relationships to their family and other people around them, but without the humor that breaks through in *The Mountain Lion.*

Katherine and Andrew both hide their guilty secrets, but each sus-
pects that the other knows what is hidden. Katherine believes that
Andrew discovered the past winter what she and his father planned.
Andrew believes that Katherine can read his intentions toward
Charles, Victor's brother. In fact, neither does know the cause of the
other's peculiar behavior. But Katherine *is* sure that Andrew bitterly
hates someone and she fears him, for extrapolating from her own experience, she believes that "within a child there lies an unforgiving
heart" (156). Andrew's torture results eventually in his being unable
to stop the chant in his head that Charles must die, with the accom-
panying fear that other people can hear the chant. Katherine's torture
results in moments of what she calls "dislocation," which on occasion
cause her actually to faint.

Katherine describes her sensations in her journal: "For I am snatched by moments of hallucination when reality disgorges me like a cannon firing off a cannon ball and I am sent off into an upper air where there is no sound and my senses are destroyed by the awful, white paining light. I know that it is only a matter of seconds but because there . . . time does not exist, it is also eternity . . ." (74–75). Eventually the image in the hallucinations changes to the image of the Catherine wheel. It had been while Catherine wheels exploded to celebrate Maeve's birthday that Katherine had discovered John Shipley was in love with Maeve. At that moment, Katherine felt herself "fixed upon her own Catherine wheel" (96). Now, her dislocations find her spinning "upon a wrenching rack [bringing] again that blinding, dumbing annihilation of reality" (96). As if to concretize the death wish embodied in her hallucinations, Katherine has her tombstone cut. Above a carved representation of herself, the stone holds an impress of a Catherine wheel, "seven hooked spikes curved inward from the rim pointing toward the name engraved there" (237).

Katherine is driven by her turmoil to relive the night when she realized she had lost John to Maeve. She plans her only large party of the summer, to be climaxed by the firing off of five Catherine wheels. When Charles, the object of Andrew's hatred, lights the fifth of the wheels, his hair catches fire. In an irony toward which the novel has inexorably built, Katherine, attempting to save Charles's life, allows her own clothing to catch fire and burn her irremediably, as in imitation of the burning wheels she runs "in a widening circle" and screams "unceasingly" (279).

Katherine Congreve obviously identifies herself with the martyred St. Catherine whose instrument of torture inspired the fireworks that cause Katherine Congreve's death. Katherine Congreve's martyrdom, however, is self-imposed. She dies as she lived, celebrating her desire for revenge against unknowing slights, against unplanned hurts, immolating her lifelong self-pity ("only the Humanist loved me" [231]). She is finally not an admirable person at all, no matter how charming her civilized external appearance. The secret guilt that she carries with her during her final summer, and which Stafford symbolizes in naming the Maine village where Congreve House is located Hawthorne, is only the final eruption of the secret hatred she has carried with her most of her life. Katherine is responsible for a terrible legacy, mirrored in the child Andrew, who worships her. In part, it is a legacy she has received from her father and is manifest in Congreve House:

> Perfect and plenteous, Congreve House was the locus but was also the extension of herself; not the events that had taken place in it which she had clung to out of her stubborn self-destruction, but the very paneled walls themselves and the wide random boards of the floors and the marble mantels and, above all, the ironic spirit of the house, mature (as she must learn to be) and indestructible (as she was despite all her efforts to destroy herself). It was her father who had imbued the house with its spirit of acceptance. (265).

The mature and indestructible ironic spirit can, however, lead to an objective detachment that allows one to manipulate other human beings, as her father has done and as Katherine does. It can allow the highest level of control while it destroys the sense of humanity.

A Mother in History

In 1965, on assignment for *McCall's*, Stafford interviewed Marguerite Oswald, the mother of Lee Harvey Oswald, the alleged assassin of President John F. Kennedy. She published an article, "Strange World of Marguerite Oswald," based on the interview.[13] In an essay published a decade later,"Somebody Out There Hates Me," Stafford describes the outraged hate mail she received as a result:

> While I had, I thought, made no judgments, allowed Mrs. Oswald to be her own advocate and her own jury, and had been myself little more than the court stenographer, the spectators accused me of seeking to demolish the sacred throne of motherhood on which Mrs. Oswald was entitled to sit. On the other hand, I had also sought to enthrone and enshrine a wicked woman who did not deserve the sacred name of Mother. I was a Catholic in an anti-Semitic plot; I was a Jew in an anti-Catholic plot; I was a card-carrying Communist; I was a member of the Birch Society. To my great wonderment, I learned that I had it in for the Lutheran churches of Chicago. I had been hoodwinked by the Warren Commission Report; I had not read a syllable of the Warren Report. I was smartly brought to book by a Democratic Congressman of Connecticut for invading Mrs. Kennedy's privacy. Several of the letters ended, "Shame on you!"[14]

In 1966, Stafford took up Mrs. Oswald's story again in *A Mother in History*, the only nonfiction book she ever published, which ex-

panded the material of the article that had excited such diverse op-
probrium. Again, if one accepts the vast amount of direct quotation
attributed to Mrs. Oswald, Stafford served primarily as "court steno-
grapher." The subject of the interview, however, seems to have been
"right up her alley," as Stafford herself might have said. Mrs. Oswald
could have stepped from the pages of Stafford's fiction. She exhibits
the paranoia of Mrs. Placer in "In the Zoo." She shares the pride and
the illusions of the lower-middle-class landladies in "The Tea Time
of Stouthearted Ladies." She is the mother of the orphan who turned
assassin. And she has been on the move all her life. Stafford captures
many of her qualities in the following description:

> Her affable face was round and lineless, and the skin that covered her
> small bones was delicate; her eyes were clear behind glasses in pale frames;
> and her clean white hair, only a little smudged with left-over gray, was
> pulled back straight into a plump and faultless bun. She wore a lime-green
> sheath that was appropriate to her short stature and her tubular, well-cor-
> seted construction. She would, I thought, be called "modish." Her general
> appearance and her demeanor were consistent with the several roles she has
> played in her fifty-eight years: insurance agent, saleslady, manageress of lin-
> gerie shops, switchboard operator, practical nurse.[15]

The book is divided into three parts, corresponding to the three
days of interviews. Stafford the novelist sets the scene for the interviews with careful descriptions of Mrs. Oswald's rented home, her
manner of dress, and her various vocal intonations. In introducing her
reasons for doing the interviews, Stafford also describes some of the
concepts that lie behind themes in her own fiction:

> I had come to Texas to see Mrs. Oswald because . . . while she remains
> peripheral to the immediate events of the Dallas killings, she is inherent to
> the evolution of the reasons for them . . . if we accept the . . . premise that
> the child is father of the man: we need to know the influences and accidents
> and loves and antipathies and idiosyncrasies that were the ingredients mak-
> ing up the final compound. . . .
> For all practical purposes, she was her son's only parent, since his father
> died before he was born and her later marriage lasted too short a time to
> have much effect on him. Relatives are often (perhaps more often than not)
> the last people on earth to know anything about each other. Still, there was
> the possibility. . . . (4–5)

What Stafford finds when she goes to Texas is as bizarre a human
being as any she ever created—a woman who says that "the Oswald
family was actually an average American family" (25), although there
is considerable evidence to the contrary; a woman who believes it
would be "just a normal thing to have a mercy killing of the President" (15); and a woman who has had the following statement cut
into a copper plaque that she displays on her living room wall:

> MY SON—
> LEE HARVEY OSWALD EVEN AFTER HIS DEATH HAS DONE
> MORE FOR HIS COUNTRY THAN ANY OTHER LIVING HUMAN
> BEING
>   MARGUERITE C. OSWALD
>   (37)

Although Stafford draws no final conclusions based on her stated intentions for the interviews, the monstrous portrait of the mother displayed in *A Mother in History* suggests the conclusion that Stafford the
novelist might have reached—the fatherless orphan sought his revenge by killing the most powerful representative figure of the father
that he could approach.

Chapter Five
Critical Assessment
Self-Critique

In the most straightforward, least tongue-in-cheek essay that Stafford published on the writing of fiction, she writes: "The novel does not exist that is not psychological, is not concerned with emotional motivations and their intellectual resolutions, with instincts and impulses and conflicts and behavior, with the convulsions and complexities of human relationships, with the crucifixions and the solaces of being alive."[1] She develops her essay by demonstrating that by this definition she was being inclusive, rather than exclusive, that it applied to all writers whom one would consider "great," not simply those post-Freud. She argues for "true endings based upon true premises, for that detachment from our characters' eccentricities and misadventures that prevents us from making them into improbable prodigies but that, on the contrary, enables us to be psychologically sound."[2] She concludes with an observation that is at once stringent and eclectic:

I do not think it matters what one writes about nor what method one selects to use; one may be altogether autobiographical or use none of one's own experience; it is equally good to innovate and to stick to the traditional rules; one may employ an omniscient observer or tell the tale without a guide. None of this matters if the eye and the ear, and therefore the pen, remain loyal to reality. Like the psychiatrist, the novelist must see his characters at once as individuals and as members of the human race; like him, the novelist must determine why they speak as they do and why they behave as they do and what in their nature causes them to react as they do to the situations into which he, their omnipotent sponsor, puts them.[3]

In another essay on the role of the novelist published three years later, Stafford writes: "I do not advocate the rejection of experience, for if I did, and practiced what I preached, I would have to stop writing tomorrow. But I do argue long and loud against the case history, and particularly the case history that is long on psychological analysis and short on action and plot."[4]

These observations by Stafford, although they were written rather early in her career, remain significant for understanding her practice as a writer of fiction. All of her significant work is grounded in the immediacy of experience, and it reaches the level of high art because as a writer she constantly explores the intensity and complexity of the human experience, the emotions and motivations of her characters, which lead to not often happy, but "true" endings. Stafford remained "loyal to reality," as she perceived it. It *has* mattered, however, that she made the choices as a writer that she did. She chose, in the main, not to innovate, but to hold to tradition. She chose frequently to be autobiographical. She chose, primarily, to write about the lives of women. And she saw the psychological reality of those lives refracted through her own vision of life as a woman, which began with her own experiences as a child in the midst of an unhappy family.

In an article on the young women who clustered around the murderous Charles Manson, Stafford takes a surprising and revealing stance. She finds it understandable that the women entered Manson's community, "out of the instinctive (although often inadmissible) need to belong to someone and to own someone, to have brothers and sisters and, above all, a father—to have, in short, kinsmen under the skin if not by blood. The horrendous perversions of the moral code and of the traditions of protectiveness, guidance, and support that accrued to Manson as paterfamilias was not just a cry for love but a desperate shriek in the wilderness. If the tale that is unfolding were not so monstrous, aspects of it would break the heart."[5] When Stafford wrote this passage, she had already published all the fiction she would publish, except the excerpts from her unfinished novel that appeared almost a decade later. The passage, although it evaluates "real life" and not "art," capsulizes the major psychological situation that Stafford explored in decades of writing fiction: "the instinctive (although often inadmissible) need [of a young woman] to belong to someone . . . to have . . . above all, a father." The need, as she demonstrates in story after story, and novel after novel, can develop from "a cry for love" into "a desperate shriek in the wilderness."

Stafford clothed the agony of her characters in a brilliant style which has allowed critics to appraise her work without coping with the particular kind of "desperate shriek" that resides there. Most have not paid much attention to the fact that Stafford mainly writes about women. Olga W. Vickery does recognize Stafford's depiction of "the collapse of the family as bulwark and wellspring" in a list of symptoms of cultural dissolution that she finds in Stafford's work.[6] When Vickery sums up her conclusions about Stafford's ironic vision, however, one would not recognize from her traditional language (which reflects traditional literary critical conventions) that Stafford's novels had heroines, not heroes:

The social world of Boston, the natural world of Colorado, and the civilized world of Congreve House symbolize three major ways in which man has attempted to escape the dilemma of his own nature. But the ironic vision forces man to look at his own image and without equivocation to recognize therein a shifting, flickering shape. In terms of action man is necessarily the victim of his own dual nature and world, but in terms of knowledge he transcends the conflict. To understand the human condition is the only form the quest can take when it is conducted under the guidance of the ironic vision.[7]

Even farther from the mark, Sid Jenson describes the conflict in "The Bleeding Heart" as "between *a man* and his environment" and in "The Tea Time of Stouthearted Ladies" as "*a man* struggles with himself."[8]

Stafford did not see herself as a feminist, and she made some rather harsh remarks about aspects of the contemporary feminist movement, which, among other things, she said, "attracted hordes of Dumb Doras and Xanthippes and common scolds."[9] But one does not have to be a feminist to see the world from a woman's point of view and to write fiction that is part of what Elizabeth Janeway calls "women's literature" and incorporates that point of view. Janeway includes Stafford as an author of women's literature, which she defines by asking the following question about the vision from which women's experience is treated in literature: "Is this experience described and judged in terms which can be various and individual but which are inherently the product of women's lives, or is it judged by masculine principles and values?"[10] Although Janeway does not discuss Stafford's work in detail, characteristics of a women's literature which she identifies are amply displayed in Stafford's novels and stories: "a concentration on lived experience," a confrontation with powerlessness, an "interior journey" that sometimes verges on madness in an attempt to determine the "inner reality" of her experience, the revelation of victimization that often results from such an interior quest.[11]

General Assessments

Jeannette Mann contended in 1976 that Stafford had received so little serious critical attention primarily because she presents "a new kind of truth," which needs "as with the work of many women writers, new structures and a new vocabulary . . . to understand it."[12] At least, the serious critic needs to recognize that Stafford is writing about women and women's lives, which indeed display a different kind of truth that recent criticism is beginning to take into account. The best case in point is the changing evaluation of *The Mountain Lion,* the novel that has received the most critical attention.

In the first critical article published on Stafford's novels, in 1955, Ihab H. Hassan finds the contrast between Grandfather Kenyon and Grandfather Bonney essential and finds that it isolates "Miss Stafford's recurring themes of past and present, of the expense of spirit, of the perpetual engagement between sense and insensibility, ideal and reality."[13] He represents Molly as merely the one of the two adolescents who refuses to change. And he finds the mountain lion, the central symbol, unsuccessful because "it lacks emotional immediacy and lacks the power to unite and reveal." He considers the novel limited because "the tragedy of Ralph and Molly is not sufficiently rendered in the terms of moral perception," and finally summarizes the novel as "the small tragedy of two adolescents."[14]

Five years later, in 1962, Olga W. Vickery discussed Stafford's novels in terms of the aliens, rebels, and freaks that she finds as Stafford's chief archetypes. In her discussion of *The Mountain Lion,* she finds both Ralph and Molly aliens and rebels, but of Molly she writes: "Clearly Molly is one of the true freaks who cannot fit into any pattern. Because she offends both nature and society, her destruction is inevitable. . . ."[15] There is no indication in Vickery's assessment that Molly's freakishness has anything to do with her gender or that she "offends both nature and society" because she is a girl who refuses to accept the strictures nature and society impose.

In 1967, in a lengthy and balanced analysis of the novel, Stuart L. Burns evaluates it from the thematic criterion of "the two possible alternatives of alienation or adaptation."[16] His conclusion suggests that he finds Ralph's adaptation more tragic than Molly's alienation:

Miss Stafford has depicted the disastrous fate awaiting the uncompromising innocent in his encounter with modern society, while pointing out that a loss of innocence and a compromise of ideals go hand in hand. Molly, the uncompromising innocent, adherent to the ideals of a vanished nineteenth century society, fails to achieve self-realization; Ralph succeeds, but only by abandoning most of his ideals. Since Miss Stafford obviously prefers the values inherent in the earlier society, both plots are tragic, but the real tragedy implicit in *The Mountain Lion* is that, in order to achieve self-realization in a changing society, the individual must compromise or deny those very qualities which constitute the self.[17]

Burns apparently fails to recognize that, because Molly is female, the options for her adaptation are so limited that they are meaningless to her.

Contemporary with these early appraisals and in contradiction to them to some extent is Louis Auchincloss's discussion of the novel in 1965. Significantly, he finds Molly at the center of the novel. He begins his discussion with the following sentence: "It is not so much what Molly Fawcett sees or remembers that is significant; it is what Molly *is,* and, incidentally, what she stands for." He continues: "She is a symbol, like the tawny, elusive mountain lion which the men *must* kill, of that virginal, childhood, uncontaminated *something* that is inevitably lost in growing up. In the end she must die with the mountain lion. . . ."[18] Auchincloss, finally, distinguishes the novel from Stafford's others as her "masterpiece." Stafford, by the way, indicated indirectly her approval of Auchincloss's evaluation of her work by mentioning his book and the brilliance of its title.[19]

In two articles, Blanche H. Gelfant has extended Auchincloss's evaluation of Molly's death to assert that Molly must die, not simply because of her virginal innocence, but because she is also female. Gelfant writes: "Her death is demanded by the great masculine myth of the West—a symbolic place: where boys like Ralph become men; and girls like Molly become not only extraneous and intrusive, but actually threatening to the ritual of male initiation."[20] Gelfant also poses an answer to Molly's own death wish, which she finds in Molly's appraisal of her ugliness. Gelfant proposes that "Molly's life is blighted by her looks; and her character is demoralized by her acceptance of society's judgment that her looks are ugly. . . . Finally hating herself for the same reasons others hate her, because she assaults their sense of female beauty, she wants to erase herself from view, to disappear, to die. Though she is precocious, ambitious, critical, and discerning, her talents go to waste; her epitaph is 'trash.' "[21]

Gelfant's recognition of the importance of the difference in gender
of the central characters in the novel is developed further in the two
most recent articles on *The Mountain Lion*. Melody Graulich opens her
discussion of the novel and of the story "Bad Characters" with the
following general statement: "Much of Stafford's fiction explores the
consequences of rigid sex roles. In her three novels . . . and in some
of her best stories, she shows the price women pay for wearing enforced social masks which deface their inner selves. . . . Stafford's
women rebel only indirectly, and often self-destructively. . . . [They]
are often too self-effaced to assert a self apart from social
norms. . . .They nurture [their real selves] in a private world of
alienation. . . ."[22] Graulich goes on, however, to make the particular
point of her essay, that Stafford's girls rebel as long as they dare
against these norms. Using Stafford's own distinctions of the "noble"
(female) and "wicked" (male) West, Graulich points out that although Ralph and Molly are almost identical in every way as children, "*her* basic identity is unacceptable, denied" in both the
stereotyped male and female worlds of the West: "Independent, al-
ienated, outspoken, and ugly, she is everything a 'noble' woman
should not be. Her very presence produces social awkwardness. Even
her strengths become weaknessess. . . . Molly's rebellious individu-
alism would seem to make her a natural candidate for membership in
the wicked West. And yet again—over and over again—she is rejected. . . ."[23] Rejected for what she is ("wicked") and unable to con-
form to the role expected of her ("noble"), she is killed off by Stafford
because "she is a misfit who has no wilderness, no territory, to run
to."[24]

Barbara A. White forthrightly states the central issue of *The Mountain Lion*—as it must be viewed in the context of Stafford's primary
subject matter:

[The novel] does not simply assume x, an adolescent resistant to initiation,
and y, an adolescent accepting of initiation, and move on to other matters.
Stafford is primarily concerned with portraying why it is that one adolescent
rejects what the other can accept. Why is Molly a misfit and Ralph a candidate for initiation? Although the gender of the two protagonists has been
ignored, it is essential in the novel that Molly is female and Ralph
male. . . . The action of the book would not make sense if the protagonists
were two boys. Stafford shows us clearly that because Molly and Ralph are
of different sexes, the conditions of their lives and the fates which they may
expect are also different."[25]

White concludes: "Ralph accepts initiation because manhood gives him privileges. Molly resists not growth in general, but growth to womanhood, a devalued state."[26]

The changes in critical analysis of *The Mountain Lion* over a period of almost thirty years reveal the importance of evaluating "women's literature" on the basis of what its author is actually writing about—the lived experience of women—and how that differs from the lived experience of men, the standard by which literature has been traditionally judged. It is somewhat astonishing how many of the critical essays on Stafford's work begin with a statement that she does not deserve the critical neglect she has received. It is perhaps because she has written primarily about women—and their devalued lives—that the neglect has come. It is not necessary here to argue that the real lives of women and the artistic work of women have been generally devalued. That argument has been made soundly and well by many distinguished analysts in the past two decades. Maybe, by way of example, it is significant to note here that in one of the major reviews of *The Collected Stories,* the two stories singled out for praise, "The Maiden" and "The Mountain Day," are among the least characteristic of Stafford's work.[27] The central character of "The Maiden" is one of the few male protagonists in her stories. The central character of "The Mountain Day" is a privileged, protected, traditional young woman who is madly in love with and engaged to a proper young man.

Boston Adventure

Despite the sometimes inadequate understanding that critics have brought to it, *The Mountain Lion* has doubtless received the greatest attention because it is indeed, as Auchincloss realized almost twenty years ago, Stafford's masterpiece. Stafford has written that Ford Madox Ford read some of her early pieces (perhaps one of them was "In the Snowfall") and advised her to stop writing so closely from her personal knowledge of people. She says: "I took Ford's advice very much to heart and subsequently I found that I could transform experience into artistic substance by the simple expedients: by shifting the scene from the North to the South or from the East to the West, by changing the occupation of a character or the color of his hair or the fit of his clothes. In his mythical environment and with his new lineaments and his unfamiliar wardrobe, my acquaintance was presently easy to handle."[28] Stafford obviously followed that advice when she wrote *Boston Adventure,* and the result was an apparent success. Not only did reviewers hail a bright, new first novel, but the novel sold and sold well.

What the reviewers and later critics praised most were the traces of Proust and James they found there. Louis Auchincloss summarizes this early appeal: "Second to Henry James, Proust was probably the strongest influence on young American novelists of the 1940s and early 1950s. It became the fashion to see his guiding hand in every reference to time and childhood. But when *Boston Adventure* appeared in 1944, it was apparent, to many of us at least, that here was a first novel that caught the very essence of the master's flavor: the continual contrast of a dreamlike childhood, nostalgically recaptured, with a highly vivid, specific study of the more contemporary 'great world.' "[29] Partly because of the very things Auchincloss praises—its imitative style, the melodramatically nostalgic picture of childhood, the detailed but caricatured presentation of Boston society—*Boston Adventure* does not withstand well the passage of time. One gets the sense that Stafford wrote what she thought she ought to write in order to sell a book. And, in fact, the book is often badly overwritten as she perhaps tried to fashion a style in imitation of the masters. Such lines as the following leap out of the text at the modern reader: "his mouth waspishly raged over my face with kisses" (145), "my heart had been skinned by his silence" (202), "her small, perfect face which disdained the pastes and pigments of the cosmeticians" (271).

The Mountain Lion

When Stafford wrote *The Mountain Lion,* however, she luckily ignored Ford Madox Ford's advice and wrote directly and with little disguise out of her own experience. She also wrote in the style that has proved to be her own. Gone are the clotted sentences and the overwrought adjectives. Gone is the melodrama of an imagined, Europeanized childhood. Instead of writing about a Boston she hardly knew, she wrote about a West that she knew intimately. She created children whose lives were made of the stuff of her own and her siblings' lives. She used the language that belonged to the West, tempered by her artistic brilliance into a language that serves the purposes of high art. Stafford has written that "language is and has always been my principal interest, my principal concern, and my principal delight. I'd rather read a dictionary than go to the moon. . . ."[30] *Boston Adventure* sometimes reads as if Stafford wrote with the dictionary at her elbow. *The Mountain Lion,* on the other hand, demonstrates Stafford's ability to find the most meticulously appropriate word, however extraordinary to the usual vocabulary, to fulfill her artistic intention.

The Mountain Lion continues to grow in reputation. Feminist critics are recognizing the important portrait of the young girl in the West that Stafford creates in Molly. Other critics recognize its stature as a portrayal of the modern West and, as such, it has been included in the reprint series of the University of New Mexico Press devoted to outstanding western novels. Finally, however, it will retain its reputation because it stands the test that Stafford herself proposed in "The Psychological Novel," because it deals truly "with the convolution and complexities of human relationships, with the crucifixions and the solaces of being alive."

The Catherine Wheel

The Catherine Wheel is Stafford's best-made novel, although it is not her best. Stafford was criticized for not fully controlling the central symbol in *The Mountain Lion.* In *The Catherine Wheel,* Stafford fully controls the central symbol, the wheel, in all its permutations from the instrument that tortured Catherine of Alexandria in the fourth century to its simultaneously degraded and exalted modern form as one of the most beautiful of fireworks. The very dominance of the symbol, however, seems finally too pat; it is overly insisted upon. It makes the ending of the novel more predictable than ironic. The novel is well made also in its paralleling of the stories of the child and of the woman. It is not, however, for its aesthetic qualities, which have been highly praised, but for its content, which has been judged slight, that the novel will remain important.

Although the main characters are Bostonians, Stafford places them in Maine, actually at the Kavanagh mansion in Damariscotta Mills, which she calls Congreve House in a symbolically named "Hawthorne." Once again she is writing about a place that she herself experienced intensely, and she peoples the novel with minor characters from that experience. She has done some of that transference that Ford Madox Ford suggested, but she has brought it off. Andrew Shipley has a strong kinship to Molly Fawcett; he also reads the dictionary for pleasure. Katherine Congreve is the woman Stafford knows best, the one whose "instinctive (although often inadmissible) need to belong to someone . . . to have . . . above all, a father" has become "a desperate shriek" not in the desert wilderness but in the equally arid and equally perverse, from Stafford's point of view, high society of Boston. Stafford does not caricature Katherine Congreve, as she did the Bostonians in her first novel, because she is writing about the woman first and her heritage only secondarily. Stafford's personal resentment toward Boston high society, to which she gave full vent in *Boston Adventure,* surely motivated her to make Katherine Congreve a Bostonian rather than a New Yorker, however. She had thereby the opportunity to show once again, but more subtly, the ugly underside of that societal apex.

The Stories

Stafford achieved her greatest critical recognition when she was awarded the Pulitzer Prize in 1970 for *The Collected Stories.* The recognition is singularly appropriate. While *The Mountain Lion* is an excellent novel and will be increasingly recognized as one of the important books written in the forties, the stories are Stafford's real life work, and all the best of them incorporate the traits of style, characterization, attention to setting and language that are found in her best novel. Stafford published three collections prior to *The Collected Stories: Children Are Bored on Sunday, Bad Characters,* and *Selected Stories. The Collected Stories* contains all but three of the stories that appeared in these earlier collections. She omitted "The Home Front" from *Children Are Bored on Sunday* and "A Winter's Tale" and "A Reasonable Facsimile" from *Bad Characters.* She added twelve previously uncollected ones; all have females as central characters. Two of the three she chose to omit from previous collections have males as central characters. In fact, only two of the stories in the final collection have central male figures, and one of these is an orphaned Indian boy. Fourteen of Stafford's stories remain uncollected. Two were published after the final collection.

Appraising Stafford's short fiction, Joyce Carol Oates writes:

One cannot quarrel with the prevailing critical assessment that finds Jean Stafford's art "poised," "highly reflective," "fastidious," "feminine." And certainly she worked within the dominant fictional mode or consciousness of her time—there are no experimental tales in the *Collected Stories* (which cover the years 1944–1969); no explorations beyond the Jamesian-Chekhovian-

Joycean model in which most "literary" writers wrote during those years. (Joycean, that is, in terms of *Dubliners* alone.) Each story remains within the consciousness of an intelligent and highly sensitive observer who assembles details from the present and summons forth details from the past, usually with a graceful, urbane irony; each story moves toward an "epiphany," usually in the very last sentence. There is very little that remains mysterious in Stafford's stories, little that is perplexing or disturbing in terms of technique, structure, or style.[31]

While Oates's appraisal is at least superficially true, she has concentrated on the externals of Stafford's art and has failed to appraise what is in fact "perplexing" and "disturbing" in the stories—the revelation of the lived life of women as Stafford views it. It was Stafford's own need "to belong to someone . . . and, above all, [to] a father" that shaped many of the stories (as well as the novels) she wrote. It was the psychological situation she understood best and deepest. It accounts for the incredibly high incidence in her work of characters who are orphans. The orphan becomes the symbol of that most bereft human state, where without the support of a family, of a mother, or most often a father, the individual, and in Stafford's fiction that is predominately a girl or woman, is deprived of one of its most instinctive needs. Or feeling the deprivation of support and love even though the father is alive, the individual is driven to seek a substitute or more often to turn inward the resentment and pain caused by the absence or impotence of the father so that a self-hatred increases the feelings of isolation and alienation of many of the characters. The powerlessness of girls and women in the stories caught in the social roles they passively play is equally disturbing. Few are able to assert themselves. When they do, the assertion sometimes takes the form of madness—the interior escape from an unbearable reality—or it is perceived by others around them as madness. They are "normal" if they accept their status as powerless victims. Perhaps most disturbing is Stafford's portrayal of the deep anger and the hidden desire for revenge against rejection and feelings of powerlessness that lie just below the "normal" surface and which occasionally break forth in action. Among the finest of the stories, both collected and uncollected, are the ones set in the West that re-create aspects of Stafford's own childhood and young womanhood. They are among the "truest," in Stafford's own sense of the writer's need to be psychologically sound; they also reveal the formative experiences that shaped Stafford's portrayal of the lives of women wherever they lived.

Nonfiction

An assessment of Stafford's writing career would be incomplete
without some attention to her essays and journalistic work. In "Miss
McKeehan's Pocketbook," an essay that Stafford developed from a
lecture she delivered as one of the Annual Rare Book Lectures at the
University of Colorado in 1972, she closed her tribute to the influence of her professor at the university, Miss Irene Pettit McKeehan,
with the following description of her working life as a writer:

> I have two studies in my house now. In the upstairs one, I am a novelist
> and short-story writer. I work there in the morning, generally wearing a
> skirt, a smock, a Windsor tie, and a wig with a black velvet bow pinned to
> the front of it. In the afternoon I work downstairs where I am a journalist,
> making the mortgage money to keep the roof over the upstairs ivory tower.
> Down there I wear denim trousers, a blue work shirt, laced half-boots that
> resemble those worn by a wardress in a Soviet penal institution, and a green
> visor. Downstairs, I am gradually accumulating a collection of essays and
> reviews and lectures and angry letters to public utility companies that I have
> written over the years, and I intend to call this omnium-gatherum "Miss
> McKeehan's Pocketbook."[32]

This essay was published in the year that Stafford suffered her de-
bilitating stroke. The collection that she proposed, if it were ever finished, has not been published. But her intention indicates her own
understanding that quite a bit of her nonfiction writing is worthy of
a more permanent preservation.

Many of the pieces are interesting for the autobiographical information woven into them. Stafford rarely wrote on any subject without including some anecdote from her own experience. One discovers
in the articles and essays the autobiographical basis of a number of
her stories. The version of the events in the nonfiction pieces, however, is usually lighter in tone than the same information when it
appears as fiction. It is, in fact, humor and lightness of tone that
most characterize the majority of her nonfiction pieces, which appeared with considerable frequency after the mid-sixties. It is also in
these pieces that Stafford gives way to her delight in combining her
childhood slang ("in a pig's ear") with the grandest of language from
her *OED*. The range of her occasional pieces from "Unexpected Joys
of a Simple Garden" to "The Crossword Puzzle Has Gone to Hell" to

"Why I Don't Get Around Much Anymore" allows one to see the whimsical element in her humor that rarely appears in her fiction.

Whether by choice or by assignment, Stafford's straight journalistic work focused on women, as does her fiction. She profiled Katherine Graham, Lally Weymouth, Mrs. Warren G. Topping, and Millicent Fenwick for *Vogue.* For *McCall's,* she wrote about Anne Morrow Lindbergh and Martha Mitchell. Her only nonfiction book grew out of her assignment from *McCall's* to interview Marguerite Oswald.

Except for these just listed, Stafford's essays and articles are almost all highly personalized. She rarely is theoretical even when discussing aspects of writing under such titles as "Truth in Fiction" and "Truth and the Novelist" and "The Plight of the American Language." She wrote in "Truth in Fiction" that "the most interesting lives of all, of course, are our own, and there is nothing egotistic or unmannerly in our being keenly concerned with what happens to us. If we did not firmly believe that ours are the most absorbing experiences and the most acute perceptions and the most compelling human involvements, we would not be writers at all, and we would, as well, be very dull company."[33] In her nonfiction, as well as in much of her fiction, Stafford revealed how truly she believed this remark, which in its context she makes appear flippant.

Notes and References

Abbreviations used in the text are *BC* for *Bad Characters* and *CS* for *The Collected Stories*. Where page numbers are not given for newspaper materials, the sources are clippings in the Jean Stafford Collection, Department of Special Collections, University Libraries, University of Colorado at Boulder.

Preface

1. Author's note to *The Collected Stories* (New York, 1969).
2. A phrase Stafford uses to describe Katherine Congreve's language in *The Catherine Wheel* (New York, 1952), 69.

Chapter One

1. "Jean Stafford on Education," *East Hampton Star,* 14 June 1973; "Home for Christmas," *Mademoiselle,* December 1951, 108–10.
2. "Letter from Edinburgh," *New Yorker,* 17 September 1949, 88.
3. Harvey Breit, "Jean Stafford," in *The Writer Observed* (New York: Collier Books, 1956), 147.
4. "Heroes and Villians," *McCall's,* April 1976, 196.
5. Breit, "Jean Stafford," 146–47.
6. "Coca-cola," *Esquire,* December 1975, 178.
7. *An Etiquette for Writers* (Boulder, 1952), 2, 4.
8. "Enchanted Island," *Mademoiselle,* May 1950, 140.
9. Ibid.
10. Eileen Simpson, *Poets In Their Youth* (New York, 1982), 123.
11. Stan Isaacs, *Newsday,* 16 May 1976.
12. Wilfrid Sheed, "Miss Jean Stafford," *Shenandoah* 30 (1979):96.
13. "Souvenirs of Survival," *Mademoiselle,* February 1960, 91.
14. Ibid., 175.
15. Ibid., 175–76.
16. "Letter from Germany," *New Yorker,* 3 December 1949, 86, 87.
17. "What Does Martha Mitchell Know?" *McCall's,* October 1972, 31.
18. Peter Taylor, "A Commemorative Tribute to Jean Stafford," *Shenandoah* 30 (1979):57.
19. Mary Darlington Taylor, "Jean Stafford's Novel—'a Superb Literary Accomplishment,'" *Bridgeport Sunday Post,* 13 January 1952.

20. William Eagle, "Lost Love of a Rebellious Lowell," *American Weekly*, 22 August 1948, 4.

21. C. David Heymann, *American Aristocracy: The Lives and Times of James Russell, Amy, and Robert Lowell* (New York, 1980), 361.

22. Stafford to Peter Taylor, October 1941; reprinted in "Some Letters to Peter and Eleanor Taylor," *Shenandoah* 30 (1979):30.

23. Stafford to Peter Taylor, July 1943; in ibid., 40.

24. Ted Morgan, "Feeding the Stream," *Saturday Review*, 1 September 1979, 42–43.

25. Ian Hamilton, *Robert Lowell: A Biography* (New York, 1982), 80.

26. Heymann, *American Aristocracy*, 361.

27. Dick Cavett, "A Dash of Bitters," *Vanity Fair*, September 1983, 126–27.

28. Simpson, *Poets In Their Youth*, 144.

29. Hamilton, *Robert Lowell*, 117–18.

30. Heymann, *American Aristocracy*, 362; Hamilton, *Robert Lowell*, 119.

31. " 'My sleep grew shy of me,' " *Vogue*, October 1947, 135, 171, 174.

32. Nancy Flagg, "People to Stay," *Shenandoah* 30 (1979):66.

33. Raymond Sokolov, *Wayward Reporter: The Life of A.J. Liebling* (New York, 1980), 278–83.

34. Ibid., 299.

35. Ibid., 310.

36. Sheed, "Miss Jean Stafford," 95; Howard Moss, "Jean: Some Fragments," *Shenandoah* 30 (1979):83; Dorothea Straus, "Jean Stafford," *Shenandoah* 30 (1979):86–88.

37. "Truth in Fiction," *Library Journal* 91 (1 October 1966):4559.

38. Breit, "Jean Stafford," 147.

39. Author's note to *The Collected Stories*.

40. "Truth in Fiction," 4560–63.

41. "Jean Stafford on Writing, Language, Women's Lib. . . ," *Barnard Bulletin*, 10 March 1971, 7.

42. Alice Dixon Bond, "Fascination with Words Started Jean Stafford on Writing Career," *Boston Sunday Herald*, 27 January 1952.

43. Ibid.

44. Author's note to *Bad Characters* (New York, 1964).

45. Simpson, *Poets In Their Youth*, 131.

46. "A Summer Day," in *The Collected Stories*, 345–59.

47. "A Slight Maneuver," *Mademoiselle*, February 1947, 289.

48. "The Cavalier," *New Yorker*, 12 February 1949, 36.

49. "My Blithe, Sad Bird," *New Yorker*, 6 April 1957, 31.

50. Ibid., 32.

51. Ibid., 38.

52. "The Home Front," in *Children Are Bored on Sundays* (New York, 1953), 125–26.
53. "The Cavalier," 30.
54. "My Blithe, Sad Bird," 30.
55. "A Slight Maneuver," 282.
56. "The Ordeal of Conrad Pardee," *Ladies' Home Journal,* July 1964, 83.
57. "A Reasonable Facsimile," in *Bad Characters* (New York, 1964), 76.
58. "Truth in Fiction," 4560.

Chapter Two

1. "Wordman, Spare That Tree!" *Saturday Review World,* 13 July 1974, 14.
2. "The Violet Rock," *New Yorker,* 26 April 1952, 35.
3. Ibid., 36.
4. Stafford once lived next door to Sax Rohmer in a New York City apartment house. She recounts that experience in "Wordman, Spare That Tree!" 16–17.
5. "The Scarlet Letter," *Mademoiselle,* July 1959, 101.
6. "Souvenirs of Survival," 90.
7. "Old Flaming Youth," *Harper's Bazaar,* December 1950, 182.
8. Ibid., 183.
9. Ibid., 184.
10. "Mountain Jim," *Boy's Life,* February 1968, 66.
11. Ibid.
12. Cavett, "A Dash of Bitters," 128.
13. Parts of the discussion (both here and in chapter 3) of the western stories in *The Collected Stories* appeared previously in "The Young Girl in the West: Disenchantment in Jean Stafford's Short Fiction," in *Women in Western American Literature,* ed. Helen Winter Stauffer and Susan J. Rosowski (Troy, N.Y., 1982), 230–42.
14. *The Mountain Lion* (New York, 1947), 48–49; hereafter cited in the text.
15. Blanche Gelfant, "Revolutionary Turnings: *The Mountain Lion* Reread," *Massachusetts Review* 20 (Spring 1979):120–21.
16. Simpson, *Poets In Their Youth,* 134.
17. Heymann, *American Aristocracy,* 380.

Chapter Three

1. "Jean Stafford on Writing, Language, Women's Lib. . . ," 7.
2. Simpson, *Poets In Their Youth,* 144.
3. Handwritten note signed "K S W" on letter from Katherine S.

White to Jean Stafford, 22 December 1955; in Jean Stafford Collection, Department of Special Collections, University Libraries, University of Colorado at Boulder.

4. Both "The Echo and the Nemesis" and "Maggie Meriwether's Rich Experience" are included under this heading in *The Collected Stories*.

5. Fragments in the Jean Stafford Collection, Department of Special Collections, University Libraries, University of Colorado at Boulder.

6. "Jean Stafford on Writing, Language, Women's Lib. . . ," 7.

7. "Note on the *Echo and the Nemesis* which appeared in a collection of stories called *Fat* (ugh!) J.S."; two-page typescript, Jean Stafford Collection, Department of Special Collections, University Libraries, University of Colorado at Boulder.

8. Stafford had used this incident and other details of the party in a reminiscence by Katherine Congreve in *The Catherine Wheel*, 143–45.

9. "And Lots of Solid Color," *American Prefaces* 5 (November 1939):24.

10. Ibid., 23.

11. "A Reunion," *Partisan Review* 11 (Autumn 1944):426.

12. "And Lots of Solid Color," 25.

13. Ibid., 24.

14. Ibid., 23.

15. Ibid., 22.

16. "In the Snowfall"; 78-page typescript, Jean Stafford Collection, Department of Special Collections, University Libraries, University of Colorado at Boulder.

17. "Woden's Day," *Shenandoah* 30 (1979):12.

18. Ibid., 16.

19. Ibid., 6.

20. Ibid., 14.

21. Robert Lowell's poem, "Between the Porch and the Altar," has an entirely different narrative.

22. The 370-page typescript is cataloged under the title of the first section of the novel, "The Autumn Festival," in the Jean Stafford Collection, Department of Special Collections, University Libraries, University of Colorado at Boulder.

23. Mary Darlington Taylor, "Jean Stafford's Novel."

24. This character is the obvious source for the Indian boy in "A Summer Day."

25. *Boston Adventure* (New York, 1944), 173; hereafter cited in the text.

26. Fragments of the sequel are catalogued under "The Parliament of Women" in the Jean Stafford Collection, Department of Special Collections, University Libraries, University of Colorado at Boulder. Cataloged with them is the handwritten outline, which is undated.

Chapter Four

1. Robert Lowell used the name but gave it a different spelling in *The Mills of the Kavanaughs* (New York: Harcourt Brace & Co., 1951).
2. Heymann, *American Aristocracy*, 360.
3. "An Influx of Poets," *New Yorker*, 6 November 1978), 43.
4. Simpson, *Poets In Their Youth*, 133–34.
5. "An Influx of Poets," 48; hereafter cited in the text.
6. "The Connoisseurs," *Harper's Bazaar*, October 1952, 232; hereafter cited in the text.
7. The first article Stafford published in the *New Yorker* was a profile of Newport ("Profiles: An American Town," 28 August 1948, 26–37).
8. "The Warlock," *New Yorker*, 24 December 1955, 27.
9. Ibid., 31.
10. Ibid., 44.
11. Stafford used a similar incident in *The Catherine Wheel*; Katherine Congreve finds a seashell in a jacket which had been given to her by a young lover in Naples, p. 45.
12. *The Catherine Wheel*, 48; hereafter cited in the text.
13. "Strange World of Marguerite Oswald," *McCall's*, October 1965, 112, 192–202.
14. "Somebody Out There Hates Me," *Esquire*, August 1974, 109.
15. *A Mother in History* (New York, 1966), 13–14; hereafter cited in the text.

Chapter Five

1. "The Psychological Novel," *Kenyon Review* 10 (Spring 1948):214.
2. Ibid., 220.
3. Ibid., 226.
4. "Truth and the Novelist," *Harper's Bazaar*, August 1951, 189.
5. "Love Among the Rattlesnakes," *McCall's*, March 1970, 145.
6. Olga W. Vickery, "The Novels of Jean Stafford," *Critique* 5 (Spring-Summer 1962):14.
7. Olga W. Vickery, "Jean Stafford and the Ironic Vision," *South Atlantic Quarterly* 61 (Autumn 1962):491.
8. Sid Jenson, "The Noble Wicked West of Jean Stafford," *Western American Literature* 7 (Winter 1973):262; italics mine.
9. "Intimations of Hope," *McCall's*, December 1971, 77.
10. Elizabeth Janeway, "Women's Literature,"in *Harvard Guide to Contemporary American Writing*, ed. Daniel Hoffman (Cambridge, Mass.: Harvard University Press, Belknap Press, 1979), 345.
11. Ibid., 346–47.
12. Jeannette Mann, "Toward New Archetypal Forms: *Boston Adventure*," *Studies in the Novel* 8 (Fall 1976):291.

13. Ihab H. Hassan, "Jean Stafford: The Expense of Style and the Scope of Sensibility," *Western Review* 19 (Spring 1955):192.

14. Ibid., 193–94.

15. Vickery, "The Novels of Jean Stafford," 22.

16. Stuart L. Burns, "Counterpoint in Jean Stafford's *The Mountain Lion,*" *Critique* 9 (1967):20.

17. Ibid., 31.

18. Louis Auchincloss, "Jean Stafford," in *Pioneers and Caretakers: A Study of Nine American Women Novelists* (Minneapolis, 1965), 155.

19. "Intimations of Hope," 77.

20. Blanche H. Gelfant, "Reconsideration: *The Mountain Lion,*" *New Republic,* 10 May 1975, 22.

21. Blanche H. Gelfant, "Revolutionary Turnings: *The Mountain Lion* Reread," *Massachusetts Review* 20 (Spring 1979):123.

22. Melody Graulich, "Jean Stafford's Western Childhood: Huck Finn Joins the Camp Fire Girls," *Denver Quarterly* 18 (Spring 1983):39.

23. Ibid., 45.

24. Ibid., 48.

25. Barbara A. White, "Initiation, the West, and the Hunt in Jean Stafford's *The Mountain Lion,*" *Essays in Literature* 9 (Fall 1982):195.

26. Ibid., 209.

27. M. M. Liberman, "The Collected Stories," *Sewanee Review* 77 (1969):516–21.

28. "Truth and the Novelist," 187.

29. Auchincloss, "Jean Stafford," 152.

30. "Miss McKeehan's Pocketbook," *Colorado Quarterly* 24 (Spring 1976):410.

31. Joyce Carol Oates, "THE INTERIOR CASTLE: The Art of Jean Stafford's Short Fiction," *Shenandoah* 30 (1979):62–63.

32. "Miss McKeehan's Pocketbook," 411.

33. "Truth in Fiction," 4560.

Selected Bibliography

PRIMARY SOURCES

1. Novels
Boston Adventure. New York: Harcourt, Brace & Co., 1944.
The Catherine Wheel. New York: Harcourt, Brace & Co., 1952.
The Mountain Lion. New York: Harcourt, Brace & Co., 1947; New York: Farrar, Straus & Giroux, 1972; Albuquerque: University of New Mexico Press, 1977.

2. Nonfiction Book
A Mother in History. New York: Farrar, Straus & Giroux, 1966.

3. Children's Books
Elephi, the Cat with the High I.Q. Illustrated by Erik Blegvad. New York: Farrar, Straus & Cudahy, 1962.
The Lion and the Carpenter and Other Tales From The Arabian Nights. Retold and introduced by Jean Stafford. Illustrated by Sandro Nardini. New York: Macmillan Co., 1962.

4. Collections
Bad Characters. New York: Farrar, Straus & Co., 1964. Includes "Bad Characters," "The End of a Career," "A Reasonable Facsimile," "In the Zoo," "Cops and Robbers" (original title, "The Shorn Lamb"), "The Liberation," "The Captain's Gift" (original title, "The Present"), "A Reading Problem," "Caveat Emptor" (original title, "The Matchmaker"), "A Winter's Tale."
Children Are Bored on Sunday. New York: Harcourt, Brace & Co., 1953. Includes "The Echo and the Nemesis" (original title, "The Nemesis"), "A Country Love Story," "A Summer Day," "The Maiden," "The Home Front," "Between the Porch and the Altar," "The Bleeding Heart," "The Interior Castle," "A Modest Proposal" (original title, "Pox Vobiscum"), "Children Are Bored on Sunday."
The Collected Stories. New York: Farrar, Straus & Giroux, 1969. Includes "Maggie Meriwether's Rich Experience," "The Children's Game" (original title, "The Reluctant Gambler"), "The Echo and the Nemesis," "The Maiden," "A Modest Proposal," "Caveat Emptor," "Life Is No Abyss," "The Hope Chest," "Polite Conversation," "A Country Love

Story," "The Bleeding Heart," "The Lippia Lawn," "The Interior Castle," "The Healthiest Girl in Town," "The Tea Time of Stouthearted
Ladies," "The Mountain Day," "The Darkening Moon," "Bad Characters," "In the Zoo," "The Liberation," "A Reading Problem," "A
Summer Day," "The Philosophy Lesson," "Children Are Bored on Sunday," "Beatrice Trueblood's Story," "Between the Porch and the Altar," "I Love Someone," "Cops and Robbers," "The Captain's Gift,"
"The End of a Career."

The Interior Castle. New York: Harcourt, Brace & Co., 1953. Includes *Children Are Bored on Sunday, The Mountain Lion, Boston Adventure.*

Selected Stories. New York: New American Library, 1966. Includes "The
Echo and the Nemesis," "A Country Love Story," "A Summer Day,"
"The Maiden," "The Home Front," "A Modest Proposal," "Children
Are Bored on Sunday," "Bad Characters," "The End of a Career," "A
Reasonable Facsimile," "Cops and Robbers," "The Liberation," "The
Captain's Gift," "Caveat Emptor," "A Winter's Tale," "Beatrice
Trueblood's Story."

Stories. With John Cheever, Daniel Fuchs, and William Maxwell. New
York: Farrar, Straus & Cudahy, 1956. Includes "The Liberation," "In
the Zoo," "Bad Characters," "Beatrice Trueblood's Story," "Maggie
Meriwether's Rich Experience."

5. Uncollected Stories

"And Lots of Solid Color." *American Prefaces* 5 (November 1939):22–25.

"The Cavalier." *New Yorker,* 12 February 1949, 28–36.

"The Connoisseurs." *Harper's Bazaar,* October 1952, 198, 232–34, 240,
246.

"An Influx of Poets," *New Yorker,* 6 November 1978, 43–60.

"Mountain Jim." *Boy's Life,* February 1968, 27, 66–67.

"My Blithe, Sad Bird." *New Yorker,* 6 April 1957, 30–38.

"Old Flaming Youth," *Harper's Bazaar,* December 1950, 94, 182–84, 188.

"The Ordeal of Conrad Pardee." *Ladies' Home Journal,* July 1964, 58, 78–
83.

"A Reunion." *Partisan Review* 11 (Autumn 1944):423–27.

"The Scarlet Letter." *Mademoiselle,* July 1959, 62–68.

"A Slight Maneuver." *Mademoiselle,* February 1947, 177, 282–89.

"The Violet Rock." *New Yorker,* 26 April 1952, 34–42.

"The Warlock," *New Yorker,* 24 December 1955, 25–45.

"Woden's Day." *Shenandoah* 30 (1979):5–26.

6. Selections from Novels Published as Stories

"Hotel Barstow." *Partisan Review* 11 (Summer 1944):243–64. From *Boston
Adventure.*

"The Tunnel with No End." *Harper's Bazaar*, January 1947, 102, 153–56. From *The Mountain Lion*.
"Wedding: Beacon Hill." *Harper's Bazaar*, June 1944, 48–50, 84–94. From *Boston Adventure*.

7. Articles and Essays
"Anne Morrow Lindbergh's Ordeal." *McCall's*, March 1973, 80–81, 108–14.
"The Art of Accepting Oneself." In *The Arts of Living*, 55–62. New York: Simon & Schuster, 1954. From the pages of *Vogue* magazine, with biographical profiles by its editors, and a preface by Gilbert Highet.
"Coca-cola." *Esquire*, December 1975, 96, 178–79.
"The Crossword Puzzle Has Gone to Hell." *Esquire*, December 1974, 144–47.
"Don't Send Me Gladiolus." *Vogue*, March 1973, 146.
"Enchanted Island." *Mademoiselle*, May 1950, 85, 140–41.
An Etiquette for Writers. Boulder: University of Colorado, 1952. Address at 1952 Writer's Conference in the Rocky Mountains.
"Heroes and Villains." *McCall's*, April 1976, 196–97, 265–67, 270.
"Home for Christmas," *Mademoiselle*, December 1951, 78, 108–10.
"Intimations of Hope." *McCall's*, December 1971, 77, 118–20.
Introduction to *The American Coast.* New York: Charles Scribner's Sons, 1971.
Introduction to *The Press*, by A. J. Liebling. 2d ed., rev. New York: Ballantine, 1975.
"Jean Stafford on Education." *East Hampton Star*, 14 June 1973. Delivered as Barnard Lecture, Barnard College, 1971, under the title "The Felicities of Formal Education"; 26-page typescript, Jean Stafford Collection, Department of Special Collections, University Libraries, University of Colorado at Boulder.
"Katherine Graham." *Vogue*, December 1973, 202–5, 218–21.
"Lally Weymouth." *Vogue*, June 1974, 86, 145.
"Letter from Edinburgh." *New Yorker*, 17 September 1949, 83–88.
"Letter from Germany." *New Yorker*, 3 December 1949, 79–91.
"Love among the Rattlesnakes." *McCall's*, March 1970, 69, 145–46.
"Miss McKeehan's Pocketbook." *Colorado Quarterly* 24 (Spring 1976):407–11.
"Millicent Fenwick." *Vogue*, June 1975, 120, 139–40.
" 'My sleep grew shy of me.' " *Vogue*, October 1947, 135, 171, 174.
"My (ugh!) Sensitivity Training." *Horizon*, Spring 1970, 112.
"New England Winter." *Holiday*, February 1954, 34–47.
"On Books to Read before Sleep." *Mademoiselle*, February 1975, 154–61.

"On My Mind." *Vogue,* November 1973, 200–201, 250–54.

"The Plight of the American Language." *Saturday Review World,* 4 December 1973, 14–18. Delivered as Barnard Lecture, Barnard College, 1971, under the title "Carcinoma in the American Language"; 19-page typescript, Jean Stafford Collection, Department of Special Collections, University Libraries, University of Colorado at Boulder.

"Profiles: An American Town." *New Yorker,* 28 August 1948, 26–37.

"The Psychological Novel." *Kenyon Review* 10 (Spring 1948):214–27.

"Some Advice to Hostesses from a Well-tempered Guest." *Vogue,* September 1974, 296–98.

"Somebody Out There Hates Me." *Esquire,* August 1974, 108–9, 156.

"Souvenirs of Survival." *Mademoiselle,* February 1960, 90–91, 174–76.

"Statement." *Saturday Review,* 6 October 1962, 50.

"Strange World of Marguerite Oswald." *McCall's,* October 1965, 112, 192–202.

"Suffering Summer Houseguests." *Vogue,* August 1971, 112.

"To School with Joy." *Vogue,* May 1968, 258–60, 128.

"Truth and the Novelist." *Harper's Bazaar,* August 1951, 139, 187–89.

"Truth in Fiction." *Library Journal* 91 (1 October 1966):4557–65.

"Unexpected Joys of a Simple Garden." *Redbook,* June 1971, 79, 179–80.

"What Does Martha Mitchell Know?" *McCall's,* October 1972, 8–10, 28–31, 120.

"Why I Don't Get Around Much Anymore." *Esquire,* March 1975, 114, 132–34.

"Wordman, Spare That Tree!" *Saturday Review World,* 13 July 1974, 14–17. Delivered as Barnard Lecture, Barnard College, 1971, under the title "Teaching Writing"; fifteen-page typescript, Jean Stafford Collection, Department of Special Collections, University Libraries, University of Colorado at Boulder.

9. Manuscripts

The following manuscripts are—with one exception—in the Jean Stafford Collection, Department of Special Collections, University Libraries, University of Colorado at Boulder, which also contains seventeen manuscripts of juvenile writings and an unfinished children's book, "Wuberts," composed with Robert Lowell.

"The Autumn Festival." Novel. 370-page typescript.

"In the Snowfall." Unfinished novel. 78-page typescript.

"The Parliament of Women." Alternate title, "The Dream of the Red Room." Unfinished novel. 74-page typescript; 28 pages of notes.

"The Parliament of Women." Unpublished novel. Manuscript held by Farrar, Straus & Giroux, New York.

"Sense and Sensibility." 31-page typescript. Barnard Lecture, 1971.

"The Snows of Yesteryear." 21-page typescript. Barnard Lecture, 1971.

SECONDARY SOURCES

1. Bibliography
Avila, Wanda. *Jean Stafford: A Comprehensive Bibliography.* New York: Garland Publishing Co., 1983. Lists, in part 1, Stafford's books, stories, articles and essays, book and movie reviews, and miscellanea and, in part 2, criticism and reviews of Stafford's works and bio-bibliographical items; annotated.

2. Books and Articles
Auchincloss, Louis. "Jean Stafford." In *Pioneers and Caretakers: A Study of Nine American Women Novelists,* 152–60. Minneapolis: University of Minnesota Press, 1965. Discusses Proustian elements in *Boston Adventure,* the symbolism of Molly in *The Mountain Lion* (which Auchincloss considers a masterpiece), *The Catherine Wheel,* and some stories, concluding that Stafford is "foremost" a novelist.
Burns, Stuart L. "Counterpoint in Jean Stafford's *The Mountain Lion.*" *Critique,* 9 (1967):20–32. Discusses the alternate paths of alienation, followed by Molly, and of adaptation and integration, followed by Ralph, which lead to her destruction and to his acceptance of a manhood in the mold of a Bonney merchant.
Condon, Richard A. "Stafford's THE INTERIOR CASTLE." *Explicator* 15 (October 1956), no. 6. Notes the relationship between St. Teresa's *The Interior Castle* and Stafford's story of the same title.
Eisinger, Chester E. *Fiction of the Forties,* 294–307. Chicago: University of Chicago Press, 1963. Discusses Stafford's novels as the best examples of the Jamesian tradition continued into the mid-century.
Gelfant, Blanche H. "Reconsideration: *The Mountain Lion.*" *New Republic,* 10 May 1975, 22–25. Discusses the novel in terms of the masculine myth of the West, the rituals of which provide an inevitable outcome for both Ralph and Molly.
————. "Revolutionary Turnings: *The Mountain Lion* Reread." *Massachusetts Review* 20 (Spring 1979):117–25. Expands her previous article, including a discussion of Stafford's social satire and her denial of any "greatness" to anything American.
Graulich, Melody. "Jean Stafford's Western Childhood: Huck Finn Joins the Campfire Girls." *Denver Quarterly* 18 (Spring 1983):39–55. Examines *The Mountain Lion* and "Bad Characters" through the characters of Molly and Emily as evidence of Stafford's questioning and satirizing the Western stereotype of "rebellious-male-and-civilizing-female."
Hamilton, Ian. *Robert Lowell: A Biography.* New York: Random House, 1982. Provides an account of Stafford's meeting and marriage to Robert Lowell.

Hassan, Ihab H. "Jean Stafford: The Expense of Style and the Scope of Sensibility." *Western Review* 19 (Spring 1955):185–203. Discusses the published novels and some stories, defining the central metaphor of Stafford's work as age and childhood.

Heymann, C. David. *American Aristocracy: The Lives and Times of James Russell, Amy, and Robert Lowell.* New York: Dodd, Mead & Co., 1980. Provides an account of Stafford's meeting and marriage to Robert Lowell.

Jenson, Sid. "The Noble Wicked West of Jean Stafford." *Western American Literature* 7 (Winter 1973):261–70. Contends that Stafford wishes to bring the "civilization" of the East to the West.

Mann, Jeanette W. "Toward New Archetypal Forms: *Boston Adventure.*" *Studies in the Novel* 8 (Fall 1976):291–303. Analyzes Sonia Marburg's conflict in terms of the archetype of the Great Mother.

————. "Toward New Archetypal Forms: Jean Stafford's *The Catherine Wheel.*" *Critique* 17 (1975):77–92. Analyzes the novel from the viewpoint of the central symbol of the circle.

Pilkington, William T. Introduction to *The Mountain Lion.* Albuquerque: University of New Mexico Press, 1977. Discusses two sets of opposites as central to the novel—the West and the East and innocence and experience.

Shenandoah 30 (1979):5–100. Jean Stafford memorial issue; includes "Woden's Day," with an introduction by Robert Giroux, letters from Stafford to Peter and Eleanor Taylor, tributes and reminiscences by Peter Taylor, Nancy Flagg, Howard Moss, Dorothea Straus, Wilfrid Sheed, and a brief essay on Stafford's short fiction by Joyce Carol Oates.

Simpson, Eileen. *Poets In Their Youth,* 115–46. New York: Random House, 1982. A chapter entitled "Damariscotta Mills: Jean and Cal" describes the visit by the author and her husband John Berryman in July 1946 to Stafford and Lowell in Maine.

Sokolov, Raymond. *Wayward Reporter: The Life of A. J. Liebling.* New York: Harper & Row, 1980. Provides an account of Stafford's meeting and marriage to A. J. Liebling.

Vickery, Olga W. "Jean Stafford and the Ironic Vision." *South Atlantic Quarterly* 61 (Autumn 1962):484–91. Cites three archetypes—the alien, the rebel, and the freak—as the focal points of Stafford's ironic appraisal of modern culture.

————. "The Novels of Jean Stafford." *Critique* 5 (Spring–Summer 1962):14–26. Discusses the novels in detail, extending the thesis of her *South Atlantic Quarterly* article, to which she here refers.

Walsh, Mary Ellen Williams. "The Young Girl in the West: Disenchantment in Jean Stafford's Short Fiction." In *Women and Western American Literature,* edited by Helen Winter Stauffer and Susan J. Rosowski,

230–42. Troy, N.Y.: Whitston Publishing Co., 1982. Discusses the Western stories in *The Collected Stories,* contrasting the restricted lives of the characters with the expansive Western tradition.

White, Barbara. "Initiation, the West, and the Hunt in Jean Stafford's *The Mountain Lion." Essays in Literature* 9 (Fall 1982):194–210. Reexamines earlier critical assumptions about the novel and determines that the essential problem in the resolution of the various conflicts in the novel resides in the different genders of the two protagonists, Molly and Ralph.

Index